MORAL
EARTHQUAKES
AND
SECRET FAULTS

MORAL EARTHQUAKES

AND SECRET FAULTS

PROTECTING YOURSELF FROM MINOR MORAL LAPSES THAT LEAD TO MAJOR DISASTER

O. S. HAWKINS

BROADMAN
&HOLMAN
PUBLISHERS

Nashville, Tennessee

Published by Broadman & Holman Publishers, Nashville, Tennessee
Acquisitions & Development Editor: John Landers
Interior Design: Leslie Joslin
Printed in the United States of America

4260-78
0-8054-6078-0

Dewey Decimal Classification: 241
Subject Heading: CHRISTIAN ETHICS
Library of Congress Card Catalog Number: 96-15883

Unless otherwise noted, Scripture quotations are from the New King James Version, copyright © 1979, 1980, 1982, Thomas Nelson, Inc., Publishers. Other translations used are marked NIV, the Holy Bible, New International Version, copyright © 1973, 1978, 1984 by International Bible Society; NASB, New American Standard Bible, © the Lockman Foundation, 1960, 1962, 1963, 1968, 1971, 1972, 1973, 1975, 1977; used by permission; and KJV, King James Version.

Library of Congress Cataloging-in-Publication Data
Hawkins, O. S.
      Moral earthquakes and secret faults / O. S. Hawkins
          p.   cm.
      Includes bibliographical references (p.).
      ISBN 0-8054-6078-0 (hardcover)
      1. Sin. 2. Temptation. 3. Repentance. 4. Christian life—Baptist authors. I. Title.
   BT715.H35   1996
   241—dc20

   96-15883
   CIP

96 97 98 99 00 5 4 3 2 1

To the rich heritage passed on to me by my two pastoral predecessors at our First Baptist Church in Dallas.

In memory of Dr. George W. Truett, pastor from 1897–1944, and in honor of Dr. W. A. Criswell, pastor from 1944–94. They are both known worldwide for their pulpit prowess, but the true secret of their lives and ministries is to be found in their hidden lives. They were both models of purity in morals, mind, and motive.

We would do well to follow the advice of the great apostle in "imitating them as they imitated Christ."

CONTENTS

Contents

Acknowledgments

*I thank my God upon every
remembrance of you.*
Philippians 1:3

Of all the volumes I have been privileged to pen, I have never
approached any of them with the caution and concern that I have
this one on the subject of moral purity.

As I look back over the pathway of my life, many people have
influenced this book. My parents lived lives of moral purity before
me and taught me from childhood valuable lessons such as respect
and character. My pastor and mentor, Dr. W. Fred Swank, lived
his life beyond reproach in moral matters, and formed and fash-
ioned my own philosophy of ministry more by what he did than
what he said. My lifelong friend, Dr. Jack Graham, with whom I
entered into an accountability relationship when we were still
teenagers and had just committed our lives to the gospel ministry—his reputation is spotless and his character is beyond
reproach. God has been so good to us. We preached together as
students on the streets and in the rescue missions of Fort Worth.
We pastored near one another in Oklahoma in the seventies, in
Florida in the eighties, and now in Dallas in the nineties.

My greatest human asset and biggest encourager is my wife,
Susie. Her love and life inspire me every single day to want to love
her more and more as Christ loves His church. Our daughters,

Wendy (in law school at this writing) and Holly (at the university), are the products of our love. We have prayed every day of their lives that they might be pure in morals, in mind, and in motive as they walk the way of this world. I am very proud to be their dad.

Finally, I owe a deep debt of gratitude to my friends at Broadman & Holman, who believed this book could be an encouragement and blessing to thousands and are making it happen in a big way. To Bucky Rosenbaum, Kirk Freeman, John Landers, Kim Overcash, and especially to George Grant, whose editorial assistance was invaluable, a simple thank you is woefully inadequate but comes from an extremely grateful heart.

INTRODUCTION

*Let him who thinks he stands
take heed lest he fall.*
1 Corinthians 10:12, NASB

Earthquakes can be utterly terrifying. When the very earth trembles and jolts beneath our feet, not only are we disoriented and thrown into panic, but the structures with which we surround ourselves crumble and topple. What only moments before provided our greatest comfort and security is suddenly transformed into a hostile environment of hurtling possessions and collapsing walls. The fright is almost beyond comprehension.

Periodically, we are shocked by the news of a devastating earthquake somewhere in the world. In 1976, China's Tangshan Province was laid waste as hundreds of thousands of people lost their lives in a series of tremors, quakes, and aftershocks. In 1985, an earthquake devastated the thronging metropolis of Mexico City, leaving tens of thousands dead, hundreds of thousands homeless, and millions without electricity, water, or food supplies. In 1989, an expectant World Series crowd was listening to the singing of the national anthem when it felt the ground beneath the stadium tremble furiously. At that moment, all around the San Francisco Bay area, bridges were collapsing, freeways were crumbling, homes were toppling, and whole neighborhoods were set ablaze by the disintegrating seismic forces. In 1995, an earthquake hit

1

the heavily industrialized city of Kobe in Japan. Millions of viewers sat mesmerized in front of their televisions, witnessing with horror the devastation that left more than five thousand people—men, women, and children—dead. Hundreds of thousands of people were left homeless and the once magnificent city was utterly destroyed.

When a quake strikes, we are helpless in the face of gargantuan forces of destruction. But, as devastating as geological earthquakes are, moral earthquakes can be even more terrifying. While geographical disturbances are relatively few and far between, it seems that moral disruptions abound. Witness the sad estate of our cultural condition today.

We have been shaken by nothing less than a culturewide moral earthquake of monumental proportions. It is the height of irony: by all counts we should be emerging from a cultural "golden age" of stability and security. It seems that whatever could go right for us economically, politically, and materially actually has. During the past fifteen years, for instance, the United States enjoyed the longest peacetime economic expansion in history. The growth alone was greater than the size of the entire German economy; the Japanese fell hopelessly behind in the most critical high technology industries: computer microprocessors, silicon chips, fiber optics, digital displays, and software; inflation dropped from 15 percent to 3 percent; interest rates fell from a high of 21.5 percent to 6 percent; twenty million new jobs were created; exports surpassed both Germany and Japan; and our share of worldwide manufacturing output rose for the first time in forty years.

Internationally, the American vision succeeded beyond our wildest dreams. Who could have ever imagined that Poland, Hungary, Czechoslovakia, Romania, and Bulgaria would shake off the shackles of Communist tyranny without reprisals from Moscow; that Germany would throw down the Berlin Wall and reunite under a democratic government aligned with the West; that South Africa would move steadfastly toward some formula for universal enfranchisement; that the old realms of Croatia, Slovenia, Lithuania, Estonia, and Latvia would emerge phoenixlike from the ashes of totalitarianism; that even the Soviet Union would literally come apart at the seams and then cease to exist altogether? Yet within the span of just a few years, this is precisely what has happened. The Cold War is over. We have emerged as the sole remaining superpower.

The strange Dickensian irony is difficult to escape: these are the best of times, but we are convinced that they are the worst of times. Despite our stunning advances and triumphs, the American people are filled with uncertainty, insecurity, and dread. Polls and surveys indicate that we are fearfully gripped by a self-effacing anomie. The doom-and-gloom rhetoric of the professional socio-soothsayers has finally permeated the masses.

If things are so good, then why do we think they are so bad?

As Christian public policy scholar Os Guinness asserts: "Despite its historic political and economic triumphs, the American Republic is entering its own time of reckoning, an hour of truth that will not be delayed. It is nearing the climax of a generation-long cultural revolution, or crisis of cultural authority."

The fault lines are all about us. The moral earthquake of our time has brought unimaginable devastation and disarray. Indeed, a veritable panoply of cultural conflicts now worry us—and rightfully so. The integrity of the family is sorely threatened. Educational standards seem to have utterly collapsed. Crime and violence are, in places, raging out of control. Scandal and corruption have compromised the foundational institutions of faith, politics, and charity. Racial tensions have once again erupted in our inner cities. Abortion, environmentalism, radical feminism, AIDS, pornography, drug abuse, and homosexual activism have fragmented and polarized our communities. The basic values of our nation are now persistently called into question. Patriotism has nearly succumbed to cynicism. In the midst of this long litany of woe, public distrust of government is epidemic, while public distrust of politicians, candidates, ideologues, and partisans is pandemic.

In the final analysis, we must admit that the fundamental shaking of our cultural foundations is essentially a moral earthquake—no less frightening than those that ravage the communities clustered around the San Andreas fault. And yet, moral earthquakes are eminently avoidable. We may not be able to solve all of the problems of this poor fallen world; however, we can do something about the tremors and quakes in our own lives. The fact is, culturewide earthquakes occur because individuals, families, churches, and communities allow fault lines close to home to go unexamined, undetected, and undeterred.

Our culture is in dire straits, reeling from the effects of societal seismic shifts, precisely because so many of us—men, women, and children—suffer from moral earthquakes ourselves. We have too easily succumbed to powerful temptations that ultimately topple our sure expectations and best intentions. Often hidden beneath the surface of our lives—like the secret faults beneath the crust of the earth—these temptations seem all but irresistible.

But, in fact, there is hope. That is what this book is all about. It doesn't offer a quick fix. There is no magic wand, but Christians need not remain at the mercy of the hidden fault lines in our lives. Even in the aftermath of terrible moral disruption, we need not simply "let nature take its course." The Bible gives us a positive and practical agenda of protection and restoration that we can—and indeed, we must—follow.

It is my prayer that in these days of terrifying disorientation and destruction you may find the immovable rock of Christ and His gospel of grace—and there find refuge and strength. It is my prayer that you will learn to make wise decisions even when all the rest of the world trembles and shakes around you. It is my prayer that you will be able to overcome temptation and emerge triumphant in accord with the good providence of our gracious God.

Part One:

DEVASTATION AT THE EPICENTER: THE CONSEQUENCES OF SIN

My soul, be on thy guard;
Ten thousand foes arise;
The hosts of sin are pressing hard
To draw thee from the skies.
—George Heath

LIVING ON THE FAULT LINE

Be sure, your sin will find you out.
Numbers 32:23

᠍ঌৈ

Earthquakes don't just happen. Instead, they are caused by things beyond our sight, well beneath the surface of the ground.

Throughout most of human history, the largely hidden processes of geological activity have been complete mysteries. But now we know that the earth's crust is composed of a number of separately mobile, ever-shifting plates. When and where these plates come together, there is bound to be a great deal of geological disruption. As they scrape against one another, long lines of disturbances—tremors, shifts, eruptions, and cracks—are likely to occur. In fact, they are inevitable.

The seams between the earth's various plates are called "faults." Usually, pressure along the fault line remains fairly subtle and stable. But over time, stress builds between the plates. When the tension finally exceeds the breaking strength of rock, a jolting rupture ensues. The earth is literally sundered, and the result can be utterly devastating.

The San Andreas Fault, for example, is the seam between the Pacific and Northern American plates. It runs through California from north to south for 650 miles. Slowly, an inch or two every year, the west side of the fault creeps northward. As long as this creep occurs unimpeded, stresses in the rock do not build up and no earthquakes occur.

However, there are numerous places along the fault line where the facing blocks of rock above the plates become fused together. Pulled by the plates below but unable to move, they gradually twist out of shape and strain builds up in them—often over a period of years or even decades. Eventually though, the rocks break apart—sometimes jumping many feet—to make up for the years when they should have been moving slowly apart. This is exactly what happened in the great San Francisco earthquake of 1906 and again in the devastating Oakland earthquake in 1989.

Clearly then, earthquakes don't just happen. They are preceded by a series of smaller seismic events along the fault line—events beyond our sight that may have been quietly occurring beneath the surface for many years.

MORAL FAULT LINES

Not surprisingly, moral earthquakes follow the same pattern. They don't just happen.

We all know men and women whose actions have resulted in what we might call a moral earthquake: prominent pastors who fall into gross immorality, successful businessmen who are caught in illegal dealings, or happy families suddenly destroyed by unforeseen forces. We look at such people and wonder, *How could this have possibly happened?* Stunned and amazed, we say, "They looked like they were the all-American family." Or, "He seemed as if he really had it all together." Or, "She was so wonderful." Bewildered, we ask, "How can this be? They appeared to have everything going for them. What could have caused this terrible catastrophe to happen?"

Despite all outward appearances, moral earthquakes don't just happen. Like geological earthquakes, they are preceded by the pressures of long-hidden faults. They erupt when the ordinary pressures of life finally expose the secret cracks in the character of a man or a woman or a family.

For a long, long while we might think that such fault lines are of no great consequence. We convince ourselves that they don't really amount to anything, that they're no big deal. So we let them go. We completely ignore their presence.

Inevitably though, the pressures of life expose the cracks in our characters. They reveal the secret faults that run beneath the surface of our lives. One day, they erupt into a moral earthquake that has devastating results upon all those around us.

FROM HERO TO ZERO

Samson is a striking biblical example of a man who suffered a horrendous moral earthquake. His all-too-familiar story is told in the Book of Judges. He was a man who had it all going for him. He was young, strong, attractive, and influential—a natural leader. He came from a good family and enjoyed all the advantages of a solid moral upbringing. Yet in the end, his life was ruined by a moral earthquake.

Of course, it didn't just happen. In fact, Samson's moral earthquake was preceded by years of little faults—faults that began so insignificantly that we might be tempted to believe there was hardly anything to them. In fact, they ran their course over a period of two decades, cracking his character beneath the surface until a catastrophic earthquake became inevitable.

So what was it that really caused Samson's failure? What was his secret fault? Many of us who have a cursory acquaintance with his story might be tempted to blurt out, "Delilah. Samson was undone by that conniving woman, Delilah. He told her his secret, she cut off his hair, he lost his strength, and he was delivered into the hands of his enemies."

We tend to make a big deal about Delilah. Almost everything written and taught about Samson and his ultimate failure centers on her. We are all too prone to think that she was his greatest fault—the root of his downfall. But in reality, some twenty years before that, a few little secret faults began to run their course through the character of his life, cracking it here and there, finally resulting in a catastrophic moral collapse. Delilah just happened to be there at the end.

NO BIG DEAL

Many of us are involved in things—sinful habits, moral compromises, ethical lapses, or spiritual accommodations—that we rationalize away as petty, trivial, or unimportant. Though we know better, we dabble in these things because we think they are too insignificant to worry about. We think that they're really no big deal—just small moral faults. Later we discover—often when it is too late—that living out our lives on such fault lines ultimately results in incomprehensible damage to ourselves and to those around us. For all too many of us, our character is cracked under the surface. Our secret faults undermine the foundations of our lives, and, sadly, we set ourselves up for a devastating earthquake sometime in the future.

We let down a few standards here, or a few scruples there, and we say, "Oh, it isn't that big of a deal." Yet, that is precisely the way Samson began. Moral earthquakes do not just happen. A man doesn't just leave his family. A woman doesn't just fall into immorality. A family doesn't just disintegrate over night. A businessman doesn't just plunge into unethical behavior in a single moment of weakness.

A kind of unavoidable domino effect somehow magnifies and multiplies the import of even the most insignificant spiritual breaches. Sin has consequences, and those consequences simply cannot be swept under the rug. Cracks in our character—regardless of how imperceptible they may be at first—inevitably cause incalculable damage.

Moral earthquakes are always preceded by secret faults.

PREDICTING DISASTER

The sciences of plate tectonics and seismology have advanced to such an astonishing degree in recent years that earthquakes are now somewhat predictable. Although unable to pinpoint exact times or locations, scientists can accurately identify general at-risk periods and regions. In 1975 for instance, seismologists forecast a major earthquake in the Liaoning province of Manchuria. More than two million people were evacuated from their homes in the industrial city of Yingkou. A little over four hours later a massive earthquake struck. Instead of tens of thousands of deaths, there were less than three hundred. In California, scientists also watch key indicators very carefully. As a result, even the smallest tremors are rarely a complete surprise.

The same is true with moral earthquakes. If we allow secret faults to remain in our lives, cracking our character, we may not be able to precisely say *when* a moral earthquake will happen, but we can be certain *that* it will happen. Next week, next month, next year, or even—as it was for Samson—twenty years hence, an earthquake is inevitable. Faults create innately unstable foundations.

The apostle Paul warned us, "Do not be deceived. God is not mocked: for whatever a man sows, that he will also reap" (Gal. 6:7). When we violate God's standards, we can be sure that we are not going to get away with it in the end. When we break God's laws—whether they are physical laws or spiritual laws—we will eventually have to pay the consequences.

For instance, if we try to defy the law of gravity, we will get hurt. If we climb up on a building and jump off, we are certain to come crashing down. If we plunge our hand into a fire, we are most assuredly going to get burned. There are physical laws woven into the fabric of God's creation. We can't break them and expect to get away with it.

Similarly, God's moral laws are not to be trifled with. Break them, and they will most assuredly break us. Thus, the Bible asserts, "Be sure your sin will find you out" (Num. 32:23). We can't violate God's spiritual laws and get away with it. We can't live in fornication, adultery, greed, bitterness, anger, or rebellion without ultimately suffering the consequences of those grave breaches.

Moral earthquakes are thus, all too predictable.

A TERRIBLE DEMISE

Again, Samson is a case in point. His story is one of the saddest in the Bible—because he began so well, only to squander every advantage and every opportunity:

> Again the children of Israel did evil in the sight of the Lord, and the LORD delivered them into the hand of the Philistines for forty years. Now there was a certain man from Zorah, of the family of the Danites, whose name was Manoah; and his wife was barren and had no children. And the Angel of the Lord appeared to the woman and said, "Indeed now you are barren and have borne no children, but you shall conceive and bear a son. Now therefore, please be careful not to drink wine or similar drink, and not to eat anything unclean. For behold, you shall conceive and bear a son, and no razor shall come upon his head, for the child shall be a Nazarite to God from the womb, and he shall begin to deliver Israel out of the hand of the Philistines. (Judg. 13:1–5)

There was a cyclical pattern in the history of Israel during the tumultuous days of the judges. The people would indulge in sin and rebellion for a period. As a result, they would fall into the hands of evil oppressors. Then in the midst of their servitude, they would cry out to the Lord in repentance. God would mercifully deliver them by raising up a champion—a judge. But alas, their newfound freedom would lull them into complacency once again, and the cycle would repeat itself.

The story of Samson is set against this backdrop. Once again the people of Israel find themselves under the fierce tyranny of the Philistines. Samson's birth is an answer to the fervent prayers of his godly parents. In addition, an angel of the Lord announces that he will one day be a champion to deliver his people from their despicable bondage.

Notice the great advantages that Samson had. He was dedicated from birth. He was a true gift of God to a sweet, godly couple. He was given a special calling. Indeed, he proved to be strong, clever, and winsome—the sort of young man destined for success in life. Nevertheless, though he started out on a godly track, he ended his life picking up the pieces of broken dreams—devastated by a catastrophic moral earthquake.

Have you known anyone like Samson? Someone who had a good beginning? Someone who was God-anointed, God-appointed, and had every possible advantage in life, yet succumbed to the shock of a moral earthquake?

Samson's experience confirms the lamentable fact that even a godly home is no absolute guarantee of a godly life. Sometimes our best-intended spiritual influences are rejected by our children. Some of us are eerily like Samson: we have been brought up in godly homes by parents who prayed for us, dedicated us, and sacrificed for us through the years; yet, we choose to live our lives along the dangerous fault lines of sin and rebellion.

OUTWARD EVIDENCES

Samson was particularly advantaged spiritually. In fact, we are told that he was a "Nazarite" from his mother's womb. A Nazarite was someone peculiarly set apart for the work of God. He was distinguished in holiness by three vows he was to keep forever. First, he vowed to never drink wine or even to go near a vineyard where grapes or raisins were grown. Second, he vowed to never touch a dead animal, because he was to live a separated, holy life unsullied by the curse of death. Third, he vowed to never cut his hair (Num. 6:2–8).

Each of these vows outwardly represented an inward commitment to holiness and righteousness. They were intended to be the external symbols of an internal reality in his heart and life. When men and women saw a Nazarite walking down the street, they immediately recognized him as a man of commitment, a man of holy resolve. Sadly, Samson trivialized his status as a Nazarite early in his life:

> Now Samson went down to Timnah as a young man and saw a woman of Timnah, of the daughters of the Philistines. (Judg. 14:1)

The Philistines were pagans. They were the very oppressors God had raised Samson up to defeat. Yet there he was. Samson knew better, but still he went. That was his first mistake. According to the story, he "saw" one of the daughters of the Philistines. Right then and there he was smitten. He made his decision to abandon his high calling and to reject his righteous upbringing— entirely on the basis of his senses. It seems that he was completely dominated by the desires of his flesh. Notice: he had never had a conversation with her. He had never even met her. Certainly, he had never gone into her home. He knew nothing about her except what she looked like.

This was not *agape* love—there was no common faith here. This was not even *phileo* love—there was no brotherly fondness or affection. Samson had never met the girl. This was sheer, stark *eros* love—it was base, fleshly, physical attraction.

ONE THING LEADS TO ANOTHER

Samson was where he should not have been—down there at Timnah, down there with the godless people, down there among the Philistines—and that led to his second big mistake:

> So he went up and told his father and mother, saying, "I have seen a woman in Timnah of the daughters of the Philistines; now therefore, get her for me as a wife." (Judg. 14:2)

He went back home and said, "Mom, I've found the one. Dad, go down there and get her for me." He was ready for his parents to begin arranging for a wedding—and he had yet to even meet his prospective bride. He was obviously moved by nothing more than sheer physical attraction.

Thus began the small cracks in his character—the little secret faults—that would one day erupt into a full-force moral earthquake. Of course Samson knew better: he was a Nazarite, but he persisted in his obstinate commitment to fleshly desires:

> Then his father and mother said to him, "Is there no woman among the daughters of your brethren, or among all my people, that you must go and get a wife from the uncircumcised Philistines?" And Samson said to his father, "Get her for me, for she pleases me well." (Judg. 14:3)

His dad said, "Look, this isn't how you've been brought up. This isn't what we taught you. This isn't the law we've lived by. Couldn't you find a believer? Couldn't you find someone who loves the Lord? Couldn't you find someone of common faith that would be able to worship with you and help raise your children as you were raised?" He reminded his beloved son, "Don't be unequally yoked." But Samson would hear none of that. He was resolute in his worldly passion, "Get her for me. I know what I'm doing. I can handle this."

Samson decided that he knew what was best for him—and thus, he rejected the clear mandates of God's law and the wise inclinations of his parents' counsel. Thus, the fault lines began to spread even further:

> "So Samson went down to Timnah with his father and mother, and came to the vineyards of Timnah." (Judg. 14:5)

Where did he go? The vineyards of Timnah! Almost without warning, the secret faults in Samson's life lead him to violate one of the basic vows of his Nazarite commitment. He was not to go anywhere near a vineyard. He was not even allowed to touch as much as a single raisin. Yet there he was, walking through the vineyard, flagrantly doing the very thing he had vowed he would never do.

The fact is, when we say no to God in one area of our lives, when we let a little fault begin to spread, we are well on our way toward a moral earthquake. One thing leads to another, and we find ourselves irretrievably on the downgrade. Thus, complications began to mount almost immediately for Samson:

> Now to his surprise, a young lion came roaring against him. (Judg. 14:5)

When we step out of God's will for our lives, we shouldn't be terribly surprised when we are confronted with obstacles. Samson thought he could avert disaster, but he actually only made things worse:

> And the Spirit of the LORD came mightily upon him, and he tore the lion apart as one would have torn apart a young goat, though he had nothing in his hand. But he did not tell his father or his mother what he had done. Then he went down and talked with the woman, and she pleased Samson well. (Judg. 14:6–7)

Sin has consequences. We may be ingenious in our efforts to avoid those consequences—as Samson was when he faced the lion in the vineyard. But ultimately, even our best efforts at ingenuity are to no avail.

One sin leads to another. One compromise leads to the next. Samson very nearly met with disaster because he was where he never should have been, doing what he never should have been doing, with someone he never should have been with. Yet, lo and behold, at the very next opportunity he returned for more. It was almost as if he were winking at sin. He apparently thought he could get away with anything. Whenever we give in to sin, we pick up next time where we left off:

> After some time, when he had returned to get her, he turned aside to see the carcass of the lion. And behold a swarm of bees and

honey were in the carcass of the lion. He took some of it with his hands and went along, eating. (Judg. 14:8–9)

So, Samson returned to the vineyard. When he did, he turned aside to revisit his narrow escape; there he violated the second of his Nazarite vows—that he would not touch a dead body. Not only does Samson touch the carcass of the lion he had slain; he actually eats from it.

A PRESCRIPTION FOR DISASTER

As shocking as Samson's blatant and flagrant indiscretions might seem, we really shouldn't be surprised. After all, we've witnessed similar patterns in our own lives. According to Solomon, "When the sentence for a crime is not quickly carried out, the hearts of people are filled with schemes to do wrong" (Eccl. 8:11, NIV).

Now remember, all these events occurred some twenty years before Samson ever met Delilah. It appears that he thought he could get away with violating his Nazarite vows without diminishing his effectiveness. So, he went on his way eating his illicit and defiled honey.

Samson was exactly like so many of us today. Carried along by the passions of the moment, he somehow forgot that actions always have consequences. Those consequences may not be immediate, but they are sure and certain nonetheless. It would be twenty years before Samson was entirely undone, but the stage was set in those vineyards of Timnah. The cracks in his character made the foundations of his life less secure. His secret faults—well hidden beneath the surface—made what seemed to be unimaginable, all too inevitable.

Twenty years later, Samson met Delilah. Then came the earthquake—and thus, his life ended in ruin. Earthquakes don't just happen. They are always preceded by secret faults.

So it is with all of us. A marriage doesn't just fall apart. It is slowly and imperceptibly undermined over a long span of time by small infidelities, by little accommodations to dishonesty, and by seemingly harmless flirtations. These tiny fissures eventually become gaping chasms. These little cracks in the integrity of the relationship finally erupt into a catastrophic quake—bringing with it monumental destruction.

Similarly, ethical violations in the workplace, the fierce bondage of habitual immorality, and the sad descent into addictive behaviors all begin with small indiscretions but end in great devastation. At the end of his sadly squandered life, Samson knew that only too well.

Moral Soundings

- Can you detect some of the secret faults that may lay below the surface of your life?
- Have you deliberately ignored wise counsel to venture time after time into the vicinity of sin?
- Have you found yourself making decisions based entirely upon sensual pleasure?
- Have you allowed seemingly innocent little cracks in your character to remain unarrested?
- Have you ignored all the predictors of a moral earthquake in your life?

2

Aftershocks

Does a spring send forth fresh water and bitter from the same opening? Can a fig tree, my brethren, bear olives, or a grapevine bear figs?
James 3:11–12

ॐ

In 1956 Princess Elizabeth, the widow of the beloved King Albert of Belgium, visited Soviet-dominated Warsaw. A chief of protocol was assigned by the government to accompany her to church one Sunday. She asked him, "Are you a Christian?"

"Believing," replied the bureaucrat, "but not practicing."

"Oh, of course," said the princess. "Then you must be a Communist."

"Practicing, Your Majesty, but not believing," he responded with a wry smile.

Sadly, that is the kind of irony that haunts many of us today. We claim to believe the gospel, but we don't act like it. Meanwhile, we disclaim the ways of the world, and we conform ourselves to them. Mere expediency makes a mockery of our confession.

It also paves the way for disaster in the future. Such cracks in our character today are inevitably the precursors of devastating moral earthquakes tomorrow.

As we have seen, the story of Samson is a case in point. Though he was blessed beyond measure, he squandered his great advantages through a series of seemingly insignificant slights and slanders. Secret faults began to develop in Samson's life. Though they preceded his eventual demise by some twenty years, they were undoubtedly the root cause of his devastating moral earthquake.

Samson went where he was not supposed to go. He did what he was not supposed to do. He associated with those with whom he was not supposed to associate. He flirted with disaster until, at last, disaster struck. Though he seemed to have a supreme knack for escaping the consequences of his sins early on, the aftereffects of his rebellion proved too much for even the great Samson to withstand.

Like the Polish bureaucrat, when it came to matters of faith Samson was believing but not practicing. When it came to matters of the world, he was just the opposite. That is always a prescription for disaster.

POWERFUL AFTEREFFECTS

In 1755, the great Portuguese city of Lisbon was struck by a tremendous earthquake. Though powerful, it appeared that the initial damage was minimal. Then, after a few moments of calm, an aftershock hit. It lasted only two minutes but brought with it terrible devastation. Many older buildings broke apart. A number of roads buckled. Several wharves surrounding the busy port collapsed under the turbulent waters. Even so, most citizens breathed a sigh of relief. The worst was over—or so they thought. The land actually stilled only for a moment. Suddenly, another aftershock rocked the city for nearly ten minutes. This time, almost everything in sight was left in a shambles. The once resplendent city was reduced to little more than a heap of ruins.

Yet there was more to come. The survivors had to face fires that had broken out all over the city. The few homes and buildings that remained standing were so unstable that even the slightest breeze threatened to topple them. As if all that were not enough, a succession of great waves caused by the quake began shattering the already decimated shoreline. Fifteen- to fifty-foot-high waves pounded into the rubble of the city three times.

Hundreds of panic-stricken people, waiting in the harbor to cross the sole remaining bridge over the Tagus River, were suddenly swept away. Almost two hours after the first tremors began, Lisbon continued to reel from the aftereffects of what at first seemed to be a rather trifling quake. By the end of the harrowing ordeal, an estimated 70,000 of the 275,000 people living in the city had died from the quake and its frightening succession of aftershocks.

As the residents of Lisbon discovered on that calamitous day, even an apparently minor tremor along a fault line can have ongoing, residual effects—one aftershock following another—that can ultimately usher in complete destruction. Moral earthquakes are very similar. They can have devastatingly destructive residual effects. Sometimes those effects are not manifested until sometime much later.

Moral earthquakes are thus not only preceded by secret faults; they are succeeded by sudden aftershocks. Witness again the sad saga of Samson.

THE DELILAH DILEMMA

You would think that somewhere along the way, Samson would have learned his lesson. Sadly though, his disappointing experiences with the Philistines only deepened the pattern of rebellion in his life, exacerbating the cracks in his character. He claimed belief in the ways of the Lord, but he didn't act like it. Meanwhile, he disclaimed the ways of the world but then conformed himself to them at every turn. Mere expediency had already made a mockery of his confession. Before long it also reduced his life to utter ruin.

By the time Samson had his infamous encounter with the temptress Delilah, he had actually reinforced his impassioned rebellious habits for some twenty years. During that time, the character of Samson had become so damaged—so weakened by secret faults and cracks in his character—that he was unable to stop himself. Even in the face of obvious danger, he had become a slave to his passions.

You see, when we allow our secret faults to continue unarrested and unabated over the years, we lose the ability to exercise even the most basic elements of common sense. Have you ever witnessed that phenomenon? It can happen to anyone. Remember when evangelist Jimmy Swaggart suffered his great moral earthquake? At the time he was perhaps the most recognizable man in his hometown, and one of the most recognizable men in the nation. So what on earth possessed him to begin prowling the streets, not far from the headquarters of his international ministry to pick up prostitutes? It simply doesn't make sense. But the fact is, when secret faults are left unarrested, we tend to lose all sense of propriety. Common sense deserts us altogether. We begin to do things we would never have done before, and the results are disastrous, as they were for Samson:

> Afterward it happened that he loved a woman in the Valley of Sorek, whose name was Delilah. And the lords of the Philistines came up to her, "Entice him, and find out where his great strength lies, and by what means we may overpower him, that we may bind him to afflict him; and every one of us will give you eleven hundred pieces of silver." (Judg. 16:4–5)

Up to that time, though Samson had allowed secret faults to run all throughout his life, he had been a scourge to the dreaded Philistines. He disrupted their reign of terror among the people of Israel and became a champion of freedom. Now they saw an opportunity to exploit his obvious weakness for beautiful women. They came to his latest object of illicit affection, Delilah, and struck a bargain with her to betray him.

So Delilah came on to Samson and begged, "Please tell me where your great strength lies" (Judg. 16:6). Of course, she didn't just come right out and brazenly ask him to betray his secret. She enticed him first by inviting him into her lair. She wined and dined him. She utilized all of her provocative allure. She broke down his few remaining defenses, scruples, and inhibitions. In that sensual setting, the story unfolded ominously:

> Delilah said to Samson, "Please tell me where your great strength lies, and with what you may be bound to afflict you." And Samson said to her, "If they bind me with seven fresh bowstrings, not yet dried, then I shall become weak, and be like any other man." (Judg. 16:6–7)

Having weakened his sensibilities with raw physical passion, she plied her question, "What is your secret?" Apparently though, Samson still had some of his wits about him and he lied to her. Delilah, intent on her betrayal, proceeded to bind about him "seven fresh bowstrings" while he slept (Judg. 16:8). Immediately after, she disingeniously cried out, "The Philistines are upon you." But when his attackers came out of hiding in the bed chamber to pounce on him, Samson surprised them all, sundered the bowstrings "as a thread of tow is broken when it toucheth the hearth fire," and then furiously smote them (Judg. 16:9, KJV).

DUMB AND DUMBER

Amazingly, Samson failed to learn from this betrayal and narrow escape. He was so smitten by his fleshly attraction to Delilah that he remained captive to her affections. The moral earthquake in his life had finally taken its toll. Now one aftershock followed another, bringing with them increasing ruin. In a very real sense, Samson went from dumb to dumber—just as we do when we become captive to our temptations.

Thus undeterred, Delilah pressed her ploy further:

> Then Delilah said to Samson, "Look, you have mocked me and told me lies. Now please tell me what you may be bound with." So he said to her, "If they bind me securely with new ropes that have never been used, then I will become weak, and be like any other man." (Judg. 16:10–11)

Again, though Samson was toying with complete disaster, he kept his wits about him and deceived his lover. Once again Delilah called the Philistines out of hiding, and once again, Samson defeated them handily. Nevertheless, he allowed the farce to continue. His expedient accommodation to fleshly desire not only made a mockery of his calling and confession, it completely undermined the foundations of his life. Remember, moral earthquakes are not just preceded by secret faults; they are succeeded by sudden aftershocks:

> Delilah said to Samson, "Until now you have mocked me and told me lies. Tell me what you may be bound with." And he said to her, "If you weave the seven locks of my head into the web of the loom." (Judg. 16:13)

Do you see what was happening? Samson had weakened. One aftershock after another had left him practically defenseless. He came tantalizingly close to telling her the truth. He had become so overconfident that he thought he could get away with just about anything. That is what habitual sin always does to us. We become so dominated by our worldly desires that we are utterly myopic in our thinking.

So pulling out all the stops, Delilah said to him, "How can you say, 'I love you,' when your heart is not with me?" (Judg. 16:15). That line may be the oldest cliché in the book. It has been used in the moral collapse of more men, women, and young people than perhaps any phrase since the Fall. Though it is patently transparent, it is amazingly effective, isn't it? And thus, like so many before and so many since, Samson fell for it. Delilah pestered him with her cloying affections and maudlin sentiments until, finally, his resistance was completely worn down and he relented:

> He told her all his heart, and said to her, "No razor has ever come upon my head, for I have been a Nazarite to God from my mother's womb. If I am shaven then my strength will leave me, and I shall become weak, and be like any other man." (Judg. 16:17)

Even in the midst of his collapse, Samson could still articulate the truth. He still understood the essence and significance of his calling. He could still stand at the sacred desk and pronounce the truth in a persuasive manner. Though he played into the hands of his own betrayal, though he left untended secret faults and cracks in his character for all those years, right up until the time of the whole collapse he could still speak the truth. Some people wonder how a man can stand in the pulpit or exercise authority in the home or take a public stand for righteousness when all the while immorality has begun to consume his mind, will, or emotions. Samson exemplified the greatest irony of sin in the life of a believer: he knew full well the difference between right and wrong, but he chose wrong anyway. Of his own volition, he rejected truth for a lie.

BLIND, BOUND, AND BELITTLED

That night, Samson's ruin was assured. Delilah cut away his long Nazarite braids—the final remnant of his righteous commitment was shorn from his life:

> She said, "The Philistines are upon you, Samson!" So he awoke from his sleep and said, "I will go out as before, at other times, and shake myself free!" (Judg. 16:20)

Alas, his demise was now complete. His moral faults had remained unexamined for so long that he was unaware of the full extent of the damages. His moral earthquake had wrecked havoc on the foundations of his life, and he didn't even know it. This final aftershock collapsed the tottering remains of his pride:

> Then the Philistines took him and put out his eyes, and brought him down to Gaza. They bound him with bronze fetters, and he became a grinder in the prison. (Judg. 16:21)

At long last the consequences of his profligate life were made evident. The great champion, Samson, was left to grope in a shattered darkness, bound in chains, sentenced to grind the meal of his enemies, like some lowly ox. For years he had flaunted his dominion over his enemies while at the mercy of his base animal instincts. Now his enemies flaunted their dominion over him while he was forced to live out his final days as an animal. His humiliation was complete.

Samson was blind, bound, and belittled. For their parties the Philistines would bring him out to mock him and to mock God. That is just what sin ultimately does to all of us if we persist in it. It blinds us, it binds us, and it belittles us. It makes a mockery of us, and it makes a mockery of our God as well.

Samson lost his strength. He lost his sight. He lost his freedom. He lost his usefulness. He lost his testimony. He lost his reputation. He lost everything. But it didn't just happen. His great moral earthquake was preceded by secret faults. It was then succeeded by a whole host of sudden aftershocks. Anywhere along the way, he could have arrested the process.

Behind the business desks and the church desks all across this nation are men and women who for years have said, "I love the Lord Jesus Christ." Yet underneath their facade are unseen secret faults—cracks in character that one day will bring about a moral earthquake for all to see. The results will be no less catastrophic than they were in the life of great Samson.

BETTER LATE THAN NEVER

The Philistines had a great feast:

> So it happened when their hearts were merry, that they said, "Call for Samson, that he may perform for us." So they called for Samson from the prison, and he performed for them. And they stationed him between the pillars. (Judg. 16:25)

Can't you see it? They had the man of God. They wanted him to perform for them. Blind, bound, and belittled, Samson was little more than a humorous sidelight—a grotesque freak show.

The sad irony is impossible to miss. Once the most powerful man of his day, Samson was reduced to practical irrelevance by his own foolish adherence to the ways of the flesh. This is what even the most trivial of sins can do to us. We think such things are really no big deal, but we are so wrong—as Samson would quickly attest:

> Then Samson called to the LORD saying, "O Lord GOD, remember me, I pray! Strengthen me, I pray, just this once, O God, that I may take vengeance on the Philistines for my two eyes. And Samson took hold of the two middle pillars which supported the temple, and he braced himself against them, one on his right and the other on his left. Then Samson said, "Let me die with the Philistines." And he pushed with all his might, and the temple fell on the lords and all the people who were in it. So the dead that he killed at his death were more than he had killed in his life. (Judg. 16:28–30).

This ought to be a warning to us all. The end of Samson's life is a solemn reminder that there are consequences to sin. For twenty years, Samson assumed he could ignore all of the secret faults that lay beneath the surface of his life, but he was wrong. He thought he could get away with a few minor indiscretions from time to time, but he couldn't.

We all tend to believe at one time or another that we can ignore our sins. But the fact remains, our sins will not ignore us.

With his last burst of energy, Samson took hold of the pillars on either side of him. He was blind, but he had actually begun to see better than he had in more than twenty years. He heard the Philistines mocking God, so he prayed: "Oh Lord God, remember me and strengthen me just one more time." At long last, he realized that the strength he once possessed was not his, but God's. So he pleaded, "Let me die right here." With all of his great advantages thoroughly squandered, Samson finally began to understand: he surrendered his life completely to the will and purposes of Almighty God.

Better late than never.

Moral Soundings

- Do you claim to believe in the ways of the Lord but fail to act like it?
- Do you disclaim the ways of the world but then conform yourself to them at every turn?
- Has mere expediency made a mockery of your calling and confession?
- Are you feeling aftershocks from what appeared to be a minor moral tremor some time ago?
- Have you ignored the shaky foundations of your life for far too long?
- Who—or what—is your "Delilah dilemma"?

–3–

INTERNAL SOURCE AND
EXTERNAL FORCE

Let no one say when he is tempted,
"I am tempted by God."
James 1:13

༖

The earth's crust is made up of at least fifteen geological plates. Most earthquakes occur along the seams where the plates meet. Interestingly, most of the earth's volcanoes are located along those seams as well. The wide arc of fault lines that runs along the West Coast, across the ocean, and upward along the Pacific Rim is thus popularly called the "ring of fire."

We know that the great destructive geological disturbances around the "ring of fire" don't just happen. They are caused by shifting tensions along the hidden faults there.

We know that moral earthquakes likewise are caused by secret faults. The question is: What actually causes those faults? From whence does temptation come?

Celebrated for his sharp wit and flamboyant manner, Oscar Wilde was a notable member of Victorian England's artistic and social elite. He summed up the attitudes of millions of people in his famous line, "I can resist everything except temptation."

Most of us can readily identify with that sentiment. It is easy to walk the straight and narrow when the opportunities to diverge are few and far between. But in this if-it-feels-good-do-it day of self-indulgence, resisting temptation is no mean feat. In this anything-goes day of ethical relativism, resisting temptation seems to require a kind of moral fortitude that is not only practically unheard of, it is certainly unaspired to. We can excuse almost anything and everything.

To an extraordinary degree, our times mirror those of Samson—when "everyone did what was right in his own eyes" (Judg. 21:25). Perhaps that is why so many have followed in the lamentable footsteps of that vanquished champion—footsteps that lead directly to the devastation and destruction of moral earthquakes.

In our culture there are no moral absolutes. The Ten Commandments are little more than a distant memory. There are no sure and secure restraints on human behavior. Why, even in the church, the idea of moral certainty—of right and wrong, of good and bad, of righteousness and wickedness—has all but disappeared.

In his remarkable book, *The Closing of the American Mind*, Alan Bloom of the University of Chicago, described the frightening effect that this kind of relativism has had on an entire generation of American students. He relates that he once asked an undergraduate class to identify an evil person. No one could. Not a single student could name someone they thought was evil. In fact, Bloom said, evil did not even exist as a category in their minds. They were even unclear about what he meant by the term. Thus he concluded that our inability to recognize evil and identify evil is a sign of grave danger to our society. Indeed it is.

Even those of us who reject the relativism of our day are too often unconsciously infected by its thinking in one way or another. When temptation comes along, for instance, our first inclination is to rationalize, justify, excuse, and accommodate. We inevitably attempt to blame someone or something else besides ourselves—in fact, we are prone to blame anyone or anything else besides ourselves. Yet in the end, we suffer the consequences of such moral malfeasance.

THE BLAME GAME

The blame game is not a modern phenomenon. It has been going on since the time of the Fall. Have you ever noticed the excuses that Adam and Eve gave for their sin?

Adam said, "The woman whom You gave to be with me, she gave me of the tree, and I ate" (Gen. 3:12). "Not me, Lord. It was her!"

Eve said, "The serpent deceived me, and I ate" (Gen. 3:13). "Not me, Lord. It was him!"

In a round-about sort of way, of course, both of their excuses contained a kernel of truth. But they were just excuses, nonetheless. Both Adam and Eve refused to face up to the fact: *they* disobeyed God Almighty. They disobeyed of their own volition. They made the choice to reject the commands of God themselves. They fell into sin. In the end, they had no one to blame but themselves.

But blame they did. Adam blamed Eve, and Eve blamed the serpent. Neither one was willing to own up to what they had done. So they looked around for a scapegoat. They pointed their fingers and said, "Not me. Not me, Lord."

Yet even that was not the worst of it. Both of them also blamed God. It was the woman God had given to him who was at fault, Adam complained. In other words, "God, *You* messed up. You placed me in a faulty environment. I was only responding to the situation You placed me in. I certainly can't be expected to overcome those kind of circumstances, can I? Look, it's not my fault, God. *You* picked her, not me. We were doing just fine around here until You decided to have her move in. It's Your fault, Lord."

Eve said about the same thing. "Look God, I was deceived. It wasn't my fault. I couldn't help myself. This serpent here is very shrewd. Devilish, even. He really tricked me. He seemed to know just how to get to the likes of me. So why did You have to let him into the garden? You should have known better than to let me be taken advantage of like that. Face it, Lord. It's all Your fault."

Sound familiar? It should. Every one of us falls into that same kind of erroneous thinking on a regular basis. In fact, that sort of argument reveals the essence of our sinful rebellion against God. We simply refuse to accept responsibility for our own foolish decisions and our own perverse insubordinations. We are loathe to admit that we ever did anything wrong. We go on the defensive. We look for someone or something else to pin the blame on. We're quick to point our finger at anyone and everyone but ourselves. We become masters at blame shifting.

FROM THE INSIDE OUT

In fact, when we succumb to temptation, we have no one to blame but ourselves. What is the cause of temptation? Is it the devil? Is it our environment? Is it our biological or genetic makeup? Is it God Himself? No, according to the apostle James, none of these things cause temptation. Instead, he says, temptation has an internal source: "Blessed is the man who endures temptation; for when he has been approved, he will receive the crown of life which the Lord has promised to those who love Him. Let no one say when he is tempted, 'I am tempted by God'" (James 1:12–13).

Have you ever heard anyone say, "Well, God created me to be just the way I am. Since He gave me these feelings and urges, there is no sense resisting them," or "I can't help it. What you see is what you get," or "Don't blame me. God made me this way"? To that kind of blame shifting, James says, "Let no one say when he is tempted, 'I am tempted by God'; for God cannot be tempted by evil, nor does He Himself tempt anyone" (James 1:13).

So then, where does temptation come from? What is its true origin? According to James we need look no further than ourselves. The devil doesn't make us do it. Our situations and circumstances don't make us do it. Certainly, God doesn't make us do it. We fall into the clutches of temptation all on our own: "But each one is tempted when he is drawn away by his own desires and enticed. Then, when desire has conceived, it gives birth to sin; and sin, when it is full-grown, brings forth death. Do not be deceived, my beloved brethren" (James 1:14–16).

Some of us desperately seek to prove that the things we do cannot be helped. We go to great lengths in an effort to convince ourselves and others that some temptations are just so great that no one can really be expected to resist them. We madly search for some kind of excuse or justification for our sinful inclinations.

All of us face temptations. Every one of us knows something of the temptation to get outside the plan and purpose of God for our lives. Some of us are tempted to sins of commission. Others of us are tempted to sins of omission. Some of us are especially prone to temptations of the flesh. Others may be more vulnerable to temptations of doubt, worry, or despair. Yet we all have one thing in common: we're all subject to temptations of one kind or another.

When James tells us that "God cannot be tempted" (1:13), he makes it clear that this universal malady is entirely alien to the character and nature of God. In the original Greek text, there is an unusual grammatical construction—something called an *alpha privative*—that emphatically asserts: God is untemptable. Essentially this means that since He is not experienced in evil, He cannot tempt us toward it. Therefore, according to the Scriptures, "He made Him who knew no sin to be sin for us" (2 Cor. 5:21), "Yet [He] was without sin" (Heb. 4:15), and again, "In him is no sin" (1 John 3:5, KJV).

James not only absolves God of any involvement in our temptation, he also puts to rest the evasive notion that it is the doing of the devil. It is interesting to note that in James's entire discourse on the subject, Satan is never mentioned a single time. Why? Because he is not the cause of temptation. In the Garden, for instance, all he did was encourage the desires Adam and Eve already entertained in their own hearts. He simply reinforced the doubt that already existed in their minds concerning the certainty of God's Word, and then slithered off to leave the resolution of the matter to them. Notice: after he had his say, Satan vanished from the scene. At the moment of the Fall, Adam and Eve were alone—acting on their own volition.

Each of our minds is like a hotel. We can't really keep someone from coming into the lobby, but we can keep them from getting a room. Just because we are tempted does not necessarily mean that we have actually sinned. Just because something pops into our minds doesn't mean that we have to let it lodge there. We sin when we allow those temptations to take root. When our selfish desires harbor temptation—that is when we fall into the grips of sin.

Of course, our desires are not necessarily evil. The word James uses literally means "a craving" or "a passion" for something. That something may be something good. For instance, Jesus used this same word to describe some of His own desires. In the Gospel of Luke He said that He had a "fervent desire" to eat the Passover with His disciples (22:15). So desires can be good. God gives us these desires. The problem comes when we try to satisfy these good desires in an inappropriate fashion—in a manner outside His perfect purpose and plan for us.

An appetite is commendable. It is good to desire to eat, but gluttony is sinful; it is a desire that has strayed from its appropriate boundaries. It is a perversion of God's best intention for us. Likewise, sleep is essential, but laziness and slothfulness are perversions of that innately good desire. Enthusiastic ambition in the area of our calling is a good desire. God commands us to work hard and to strive for excellence and success in all that we put our hands to do, but greed, materialism, and compulsive overwork are sinful perversions of that good desire. Even the desire for sex is a beautiful, holy, and wholesome desire when it is placed inside the holy bounds of the marriage relationship. God gives us this pure and delightful desire, but when we attempt to satisfy the desire He has given us in any other manner or fashion, we pollute its sanctity.

There are many in our day—committed secularists, like the former surgeon general, Jocelyn Elders—who point their fingers at us when we talk about moral absolutes and berate conservative Christians for some imagined offense of oppressive bigotry or narrow Victorianism. They charge that we don't like sex enough for their taste. They accuse us of clutching at sundry arcane phobias and taboos. The fact is, we are simply realistic enough to admit that we are all too prone to twist and pervert the very good and natural desires God gives us.

According to James, when this internal source—this very good and natural desire—attaches itself to an evil object, then, and only then, is our temptation consummated. We are "drawn away" (James 1:14). In the original Greek text, this is a single compound word from the preposition meaning "out of" and the verb meaning "to be pulled away by some power." Sin occurs when we are drawn out of our place of security by natural desires fixed upon some unnatural end.

Notice that James asserts that this is an entirely personal matter. He says "each one" is tempted when this sequence begins to unfold. We all know something of this internal source, these desires within us. Each of us is responsible. We cannot blame God. We cannot blame the devil. We cannot blame situations or circumstances. What draws us away are our own desires attempting to operate outside the boundaries God established for us in His Word. We are tempted when each of us allows our desires to draw us away.

Knowing this, David prayed: "Search me, oh God, and know my heart. . . . and see if there is any wicked way in me, and lead me in the way everlasting" (Ps. 139:23–24).

David was not so concerned about worldly entanglements or demonic deceptions. Instead, he knew that it was his own wickedness that would inevitably cause him the most difficulty. "In me," that is where he looked for the root and cause of his temptation.

Knowing the internal source of our temptations, may we all pray with him, "Know my heart, examine me. See if there is anything in my desires that are outside Your perfect plan and purpose for my life."

FROM THE OUTSIDE IN

Temptation emanates from an internal source—from the desires that are within us. It must then connect with something outside us—an external force—for sin to be consummated.

There is an internal source—desire. "Each one is tempted when he is drawn away by his own desires." But there is more. James says after we are drawn away, we are "enticed." So there is both an internal source and an external force. When this internal force connects with the external force, "Then, when desire has conceived, it gives birth to sin; when it is full-grown, brings forth death" (1:15).

The word translated "enticed" here literally means "bait." Have you ever heard the expression, "He is hooked on sex" or "She is hooked on drugs"? This is actually where it comes from. When we allow ourselves to be drawn away and enticed—when we take the bait—we inevitably get hooked.

At home in my study, I have a big-mouthed black bass mounted and hanging on the wall. Years ago when I went out on the lake with all of my fishing gear, I knew I wanted to hook a big bass; yet, I was shrewd enough to know that a bass would not be the least bit interested in a bare metal hook dropped into the water. Therefore, I disguised the hook. I put a lure on the end of my line—it looked just like a worm—and I deceived that bass. I fooled him. I let my line down in the lake right where I thought that the fish would be—in a hole near a bunch of brush. Then I just jiggled my lure there in front of the hole. All of a sudden that bass saw what appeared to be a beautiful, fat, delicious worm—right in front of him. He had an inward desire that drew him out of his place of security. Then, when this external force—

my alluring deception—came along, it was more than the fish could handle.

He took the bait and was hooked. No one took the worm and the hook and put it in the fish's mouth. Instead, he came out of the hole because of his own desire. When he saw that deception, he bit it.

Now realize, moral failure—the catastrophe of a moral earthquake—doesn't start with the bait. It doesn't start with the deception. It starts with desire. Before the external force can exert any potency, it must connect with an internal source.

There were an awful lot of bass in the lake the day I caught mine. I'd been fishing all day and had dropped that lure in front of scores, maybe even hundreds, of other fish. But only one took the bait. Only one was enticed and hooked.

That is *always* the way temptation works: in the garden of Eden, during the time of Samson, throughout ancient Israel, during the time of Christ, and today in modern America. When we grab the hidden bait, the hook grabs us. The hook is not sin; it is sin's penalty. Sin takes place when my desire and some deception connect. That is why the psalmist exhorted, "Delight yourself also in the Lord, and He will give you the desires of your heart" (Ps. 37:4). We are to make sure that the desires in our lives are lined up with the Word of God.

All of this has a very practical import. The fact is, we could shut down every den of iniquity in this land—the gambling casinos, the houses of prostitution, the lurid night clubs, the crack houses, the chop shops—and we still would not be able to eliminate temptation and sin. After all, Adam and Eve fell while living in a perfect environment—Eden. There were no porno shops, no corner bars, no bookie operations, and no abortion clinics. They didn't have cable television, rock music, or teen peer pressure to contend with. They lived in a perfect environment, yet they succumbed to temptation—they suffered a moral earthquake of monumental proportions. Why? Because temptation has an internal source. It comes from within. The external forces are only secondary entice-ments to sin. The problem begins in the human heart.

As important as reforming our neighborhoods, communities, and cities may be, such efforts only offer us temporary relief from the ravages of sin. Permanent solutions are found only as people have their hearts transformed by the power of Jesus Christ—as they are transformed from within.

The real problem is that man needs a new nature. We can close down everything that's immoral, illicit, and perverse, yet immoral-ity, illicitness, and perversity will still exist. The problem with man is still his heart.

It is not a sin to see the baited hook. It is not a sin to be tempted. In fact, even Jesus was tempted: He was "in all points tempted, as we are, yet without sin" (Heb. 4:15). Sin is born only when the internal source of desire and the external force of entice-ment draw us away from that which is good and right and true. Sin is conceived only when our hungers and appetites drive us to take the bait.

Two men were walking down the street, side by side. One of those men had risen that morning and fed on the Word of God. As a result, he lined up his day within the parameters of God's will. The man walking next to him fed his mind over the previous weekend on pornography, filthy videos, and perverse magazines. When the men passed a certain corner in the city, they both came face-to-face with an enticement, a baited hook—a hooker. She smiled at both men and gave them an unmistakable look. Both men saw the bait. One took it. The other walked by on the other side of the street. One suffered a horrific moral earthquake. The other escaped altogether.

What made the difference? It came from within. One man had the grace-provocated desire to stay within the purpose and plan of God for his life. The other had allowed his good desires to be per-verted over time.

Which one are you?

Moral Soundings

- Have you been playing the blame game when it comes to sin and temptation in your life?
- Have you allowed good and natural desires to be twisted out of their God-ordained boundaries?
- Are your desires drawing you away from the will and way of God?
- Have you made yourself vulnerable to the enticements of the world around you?
- Are you, even now, laying the groundwork for a terrible moral earthquake?

–4–

ROOT, SHOOT, AND FRUIT

When desire has conceived, it gives birth to sin,
and sin, when it is full-grown, brings forth death.
Do not be deceived, my beloved brethren.
James 1:15–16

In the past decade, earthquakes have caused untold billions of dollars of damage. Insurance estimates from the 1989 California quake were originally in the $2- to $3-billion range, but by the time the massive reconstruction of roads, bridges, commercial properties, and residences was completed, claims ranged upwards of $5 billion. The 1992 quake along the Belgian, Dutch, and German borders was almost that costly. The 1995 quake along the Siberian coast down to Japan may turn out to be twice as expensive due to severe damage to Russia's military and petrochemical installations and Japan's heavy industrial concentrations there.

Of course, the ultimate costs of an earthquake cannot be measured in dollars and cents. No price can be put on even a single human life lost in a natural disaster. And yet, widespread loss of life is the all-too-typical effect of quakes.

Sadly, the same is true of moral earthquakes. Death is the tragic consequence of a spiritual and ethical breakdown. "The wages of sin is death" (Rom. 6:23).

The apostle James illustrates this principle using an analogy from the world of biology rather than geology, but the pattern he describes is precisely the same. He says that temptation is like a weed that grows in your garden. It has three parts to it: a root, a shoot, and a fruit.

The root of temptation—as we have seen—is a "selfish desire." When our desire has conceived, it grows and matures until it "gives birth to sin." At that point, the shoot appears—a sinful action or decision. Finally, if we let that shoot remain untouched, it inevitably produces fruit—a seed pod that will reproduce the cycle again and again into perpetuity. The fruit is the most dastardly of all the consequences of sin because "when it's full-grown, it brings forth death."

THE THANATOS SYNDROME

The *Didache* is a compilation of practical apostolic moral teachings that appeared sometime at the end of the first century; it is one of the earliest documents we have from the life and teaching of the early church apart from the Scriptures. It opens, "There are two ways: the way of life and the way of death, and the difference between these two ways is great."

Sadly, because all men without exception are sinners, one of the most fundamental factors in understanding anthropology is the *thanatos* factor—a phrase from the Greek that literally means "the death factor." Quite simply, it means that because of their sin, all men have morbidly embraced death (see Rom. 5:12).

At the Fall, mankind was suddenly destined for death (see Jer. 15:2). We were all at that moment bound into a covenant with death (see Isa. 28:15). "There is a way that seems right to a man, but its end is the way of death" (Prov. 14:12; 16:25).

Whether we know it or not, we have all chosen death (see Jer. 8:3). It has become our shepherd (see Ps. 49:14). Our minds are fixed on it (see Rom. 8:6), our hearts pursue it (see Prov. 21:6), and our flesh is ruled by it (see Rom. 8:2). We dance to its cadences (see Prov. 2:18) and descend to its chambers (see

Prov. 7:27). "All have sinned and fall short of the glory of God" (Rom. 3:23). In fact:

> *There is none righteous, no, not even one;*
> *There is none who understands;*
> *There is none who seeks after God.*
> *They have all turned aside;*
> *They have together become unprofitable;*
> *There is none who does good, no, not one.*
> *Their throat is an open tomb;*
> *With their tongues they have practiced deceit;*
> *The poison of asps is under their lips;*
> *Whose mouth is full of cursing and bitterness;*
> *Their feet are swift to shed blood;*
> *Destruction and misery are in their ways;*
> *And the way of peace they have not known;*
> *There is no fear of God before their eyes. (Rom. 3:10–18)*

And, "All those who hate [God] love death" (Prov. 8:36).

It is no wonder then that such things as murder, terrorism, abortion, euthanasia, and even infanticide have always been a normal and natural part of human relations. Since the dawning of time, men have contrived ingenious diversions to satisfy their fallen passions. Killing has always been chief among them.

Virtually every culture in antiquity was stained with the blood of innocent children. Unwanted infants in ancient Rome were abandoned outside the city walls to die from exposure to the elements or from the attacks of wild foraging beasts. Greeks often gave their pregnant women harsh doses of herbal or medicinal abortifacients. Persians developed highly sophisticated surgical curette procedures. Chinese women tied heavy ropes around their waists so excruciatingly tight that they either aborted or passed into unconsciousness. Ancient Hindus and Arabs concocted chemical pessaries—abortifacients that were pushed or pumped directly into the womb through the birth canal. Primitive Canaanites threw their children onto great flaming pyres as a sacrifice to their god Molech. Polynesians subjected their pregnant women to onerous tortures—their abdomens beaten with large stones or hot coals heaped upon their bodies. Japanese women straddled boiling cauldrons of parricidal brews. Egyptians disposed of their unwanted children by disemboweling and dismembering them shortly after birth—their collagen was then ritually harvested for the manufacture of cosmetic creams. We often think of such things as modern innovations in the affairs of men and nations. Nothing could be further from the truth.

None of the great minds of the ancient world—from Plato and Aristotle to Seneca and Quintilian, from Pythagoras and Aristophanes to Livy and Cicero, from Herodotus and Thucidides to Plutarch and Euripides—disparaged such brutalities in any way. In fact, most of them actually recommended it. They callously discussed various methods and procedures of eliminating the unwanted or undesired portions of the populace. They casually debated their sundry legal ramifications. They tossed lives like dice.

Actually, abortion and infanticide were so much a part of ancient human societies that they provided the primary literary *liet motif* in popular traditions, stories, myths, fables, and legends.

The founding of Rome was, for instance, presumed to be the happy result of the abandonment of children. According to the story, a vestal virgin who had been raped bore twin sons, Romulus and Remus. The harsh Etruscan monarch Amulius ordered them exposed on the Tiber River. Left in a basket which floated ashore, they were found by a she-wolf and suckled by her. Later, a shepherd discovered them and took them home to his wife, and the kindly couple brought them up as their own. Romulus and Remus would later establish the city of Rome on the seven hills near the place of their rescue.

Oedipus was presumed to be an abandoned child who was also found by a shepherd and later rose to greatness. Ion, the eponymous monarch in ancient Greece, miraculously lived through an abortion, according to tradition. Cyrus, the founder of the Persian empire, was supposedly a fortunate survivor of infanticide. According to Homer's legend, Paris, whose amorous indiscretions started the Trojan War, was also a victim of abandonment. Telephus, the king of Mysia in Greece, and Habius, ruler of the Cunetes in Spain, had both been exposed as children according to various folk tales. Jupiter, chief god of the Olympian pantheon, himself had been abandoned as a child. He in turn exposed his twin sons, Zethus and Amphion. Similarly, other myths related that Poseidon, Aesculapius, Hephaistos, Attis, and Cybele had all been abandoned to die.

Because the men and women of antiquity had been mired by the minions of sin and death, it was as natural as the change of seasons for them to indulge in various forms of killing. They believed it was just and good and right, but they were wrong. Dreadfully wrong.

Life is God's gift. It is His gracious endowment upon the created order. The earth is literally teeming with life (see Gen. 1:20; Lev. 11:10; 22:5; Deut. 14:9), and the crowning glory of this sacred teeming is man himself (see Gen. 1:26–30; Ps. 8:1–9). To violate the sanctity of this magnificent endowment is to fly in the face of all that is holy, just, and true (see Jer. 8:1–17; Rom. 8:6).

To violate the sanctity of life is to invite judgment, retribution, and anathema (see Deut. 30:19–20). It is to solicit devastation, imprecation, and destruction (see Jer. 21:8–10).

Sadly, since death-dealing is so much a part of the character of fallen man, none of us can actually change our predilections or inclinations ourselves. We are hopelessly ensnared.

But the Lord God, who is the giver of life (see Acts 17:25), the fountain of life (see Ps. 36:9), the defender of life (see Ps. 27:1), the prince of life (see Acts 3:15), and the restorer of life (see Ruth 4:15), did not leave men to languish hopelessly in the clutches of sin and death. He not only sent us the message of life (see Acts 5:20) and the words of life (see John 6:68); He sent us the light of life as well (see John 8:12). He sent us His only begotten Son—the life of the world (see John 6:51)—to break the bonds of death (see 1 Cor. 15:54–56), to "taste death for everyone" (Heb. 2:9). Jesus actually "abolished death" for our sakes (2 Tim. 1:10) and offered us new life (see John 5:21). "For God so loved the world, that he gave His only begotten Son, that whosoever believeth in him should not perish, but have everlasting life" (John 3:16, KJV).

In Christ, God has afforded us the opportunity to choose between the two ways the *Didache* posited: to choose between fruitful and teeming life on the one hand, and barren and impoverished death on the other (see Deut. 30:19).

Apart from Christ it is not possible to escape the snares of sin and death (see Col. 2:13). On the other hand: "If anyone is in Christ, he is a new creation; old things have passed away; behold, all things have become new" (2 Cor. 5:17).

Though all those who hate Christ "love death" (Prov. 8:36); all those who receive Christ are made the "aroma of life" (2 Cor. 2:16).

The primary conflict in temporal history always has been and always will be the struggle for life and truth against the natural inclinations of all men everywhere. Thanks be to God, there is a way of escape from these bonds of destruction. In Christ, there is hope. In Him there is life—both temporal and eternal. In Him there is liberty and justice. In Him there is an antidote to the *thanatos* factor. In Him, and in Him alone, there is an answer to the ages long dilemma of the dominion of death.

MISSING THE MARK

The Greeks had three very different ways of defining and describing the word we normally translate as "sin." Physically, it was used of an archer who draws a bow and shoots at a target. Though he lets the arrow fly, he is woefully short. The arrow misses the target: it misses the mark.

The word was used not only in the physical realm, but in the mental realm as well. It portrayed a student who takes a test and then comes to a tough question. Though he gives it all he has, he misses it altogether. He doesn't know the answer, and the best he can muster is a wild guess.

Finally, the word is used in the spiritual realm to describe a man who knows and understands a high standard of spiritual attainment, but he is unable to personally experience it. He falls short of it.

Thus, in every dimension, to sin literally means to "miss the mark." No matter how hard we try, no matter how proficient we become, there will always be a shortfall. We simply cannot hit the target; we can't answer the test; we can't live up to the standard; and "sin, when it is full-grown, brings forth death." There is simply no way around it.

Death—not just physical death, but the death of dreams, the death of relationships, the death of ambition, the death of reputation, the death of everything that's good—is the result of sin.

People indulge in various sins because, ultimately, they think it will make them happy. People sin because of the pleasure that it brings, but the pleasure is furtive and passing—it lasts only a moment. It is a mist, a vapor, an insubstantial illusion that quickly passes into the permanence of pain, suffering, and death.

WEEDING THE GARDEN

So, how do we go about dealing with temptation and sin? How can we actually get rid of temptation? The answer is: the same way we get rid of weeds in the vegetable plot in the back yard.

Some gardeners cut off the fruit, thinking that once the reproductive ability of the weed has been diminished, the rest will go away eventually. Though that appears to be an effective strategy for a day or two, over time it fails to control the growth or the spread of the weed at all. Similarly, when we try to deal with sin tendencies by addressing only the most visible aspects of the problem, it is not likely that much headway will be made. No matter how many resolutions we make, no matter how many times we turn over a new leaf, or pledge to write a new chapter in our lives, before we know it we're right back in our same old routine, slipping back into our comfortable patterns. Because we're dealing with fruits—with externals rather than getting to the root of the problem— sin stubbornly persists.

Some gardeners, on the other hand, take out the lawn mower and mow down the weeds, cutting them off right at the ground. This strategy aims to get both the fruit and the shoot. Although this tactic can make the garden look wonderful for a while, once again we've merely dealt with externals.

Ultimately, the only way to deal with temptation is to dig up the root. To eradicate perpetual, habitual sin in our lives, we must deal with our innate selfish desires. The only way to do that is to let God uproot our entire confidence in the flesh. In short, God must change our desires and give us a new nature.

That is why the ultimate hope of America is not in legislation. It is in each of us individually finding Jesus Christ as our personal Savior. The hope for America is not a revival of "family values," as wonderful as those may be. It is not a full restoration of constitutional law. It is not a renewed respect for women, children, the needy, and the oppressed. It is not the upgrading of the educational system, the health care delivery system, or the global trading system of the World Trade Association. It is Jesus Christ.

When we come to trust Christ as our personal Savior, He gives us a brand new set of desires. Things we used to enjoy, we no longer like to do; things we thought we'd never like to do, we find our greatest joy in doing. In short, He changes our want-tos.

So, where are you today? Are you still mired in the snares of death and destruction? Are your desires still controlling your life and work, your faith and practice, your vision and calling?

Most of us desire to exercise control over our lives. We want to do whatever it is that we are going to do entirely ourselves. We want autonomy. We want liberty. We want absolute freedom. Thus, we demand our rights and press for still greater levels of individual control. The problem is, we cannot control our own sin nature. Rather, our sin nature controls us. We are under its dominion—and its dominion is the awful domain of death. In fact, as the great reformer Martin Luther put it, we are strapped with a "bondage of the will."

Thus, if there is to be any hope that the root problems of our lives, the compulsive desires of our hearts, and the poverty of our souls are to be in any substantive way answered, it will have to be Christ doing the answering. We can't do it ourselves.

Moral Soundings

- How have you attempted to deal with temptation in the past?
- Have you focused primarily on the fruit, the shoot, or the root of the problem?
- Have you been so blinded by the passing pleasures of your sin that you've missed its real import?
- Have you ever witnessed the progression of the *thanatos* syndrome in the lives of others?
- Have you ever yielded the compelling desires of your heart entirely to Christ?

Part Two:

Opportunity on the Brink: Resisting Temptation

Yield not to temptation, for yielding is sin;
Each victory will help you some other to win;
Fight manfully onward, dark passions subdue,
Look ever to Jesus, He'll carry you through.
—*Horatio Palmer*

FIGHT AND FLIGHT

Flee sexual immorality.
Every sin that a man does is outside the body,
but he who commits sexual immorality
sins against his own body.
1 Corinthians 6:18

ॐ

Theoretically, an earthquake can happen almost anywhere. Although this statement seems to defy what we know about plate tectonics, it is true. The facts speak for themselves. In 1818, a violent quake shook Missouri. In 1886, another struck South Carolina. In 1988, another ripped through Australia's Northern Territory; and in 1990, one hit Britain. As far as geophysicists can tell, there are no active plate boundaries in any of these areas. They theorize that instability well below the top layer of the earth's crust—undetectable faults far deeper than the plate boundaries—may be the cause of this rare form of subduction.

The one solace of such phenomena is that they are, after all, rare. Even though it is *possible* for an earthquake to occur anywhere, it is far from *probable*. In fact, the vast majority of earthquakes occur along predictable fault lines along plate boundaries. They always have and they always will.

Moral earthquakes follow a similar pattern. Though it is possible for a moral earthquake to be caused by the most inconsequential moral faults, it is more likely to be caused by more predictable faultlines. In fact, the vast majority of moral earthquakes are caused by greed, avarice, bitterness, and, of course, sexual promiscuity.

Sex. We are consumed by it. We are immersed in it. We can hardly escape its smothering influences. Our entire pop culture seems to revolve around it. Yet our obsession has hardly brought us satisfaction. On the contrary, it has brought untold suffering and destruction.

It is ironic that our sophisticated society cannot see that sexual immorality has devastated our culture. The evidence is glaring: millions of illegitimate births, the highest divorce rate in the world, rampant sexually transmitted diseases—including AIDS—not to mention an unchecked abortion industry that not only victimizes preborn children, it haunts millions of women with the plague of post-abortion syndrome.

Yet we are continually bombarded with sex, sex, and more sex. We can't pick up a newspaper, a magazine, turn on a television set, go to a movie, or see an advertisement without salvos of innuendo, bravado, and libido. Sex sells in America. It sells blue jeans. It sells music. It sells mouthwash. It sells everything: cars, computers, and cameras. As a result, yesterday's shocking behavior is quite commonplace today.

What just a generation ago was forced to slither down the back alleys of America now parades proudly down main street—often promoted by the highest offices in the land. Consider the messages sent by the White House to the teenagers of America in recent years. On inauguration day, 1993, the president took his twelve-year-old daughter and dropped her off at the MTV ball. He and his wife then ended their big night at the gay ball. The next day, he lauded several of his most brazen appointees to high positions of authority in the administration. From the start, they promoted a host of outrageous positions regarding sexual immorality. The AIDS czar, for instance, said that he thinks America is a repressed, Victorian society and recommended that the populous, including teens, seek ever-increasing pleasure in unrestrained sex.

Another appointee sought to require value-free sex education for all of America's children beginning in kindergarten. She said that since they have been educated about what to do in the front seat; they ought to also know what to do in the back seat. She derided conservative Christians by saying we didn't enjoy sex enough and needed to get over our "love affair with the fetus."

To make matters worse, we've raised a generation of young people, by and large, with no moral absolutes and no spiritual leadership at home or in the church. Almost everyone talks to them about sex—except moms and dads and pastors. Consequently, a generation of kids have learned about it from Madonna and the media, from public education and the Dr. Ruths of this world who fill their young minds with misinformation and half-truths.

In the church, these young people have stood by and watched as we steadfastly avoided addressing the most critical issues of our day. At the same time, however, they observed all too many high-profile leaders of the church fall into sexual sins.

Is it any wonder that so many young people succumb to these sexual pressures and temptations when the home, the church, and the nation fail to give them the moral support they need? We've raised a generation without moral absolutes because in school, at home, and in the church our young people are not hearing the whole story. There's only one way to have safe sex: the Bible way.

America is in the midst of moral collapse and we're asking, "What should we do about it?" Many say, "More education. Distribute condoms. Find a cure." However, what we really ought to be asking is *why?* Why are we standing idly by watching our culture fall into decay and disintegration?

The apostle Paul confronted this issue head on when he wrote to a church of men and women living in a society in every way as perverted as ours. He didn't back away from this indelicate subject—because he knew how important it was. He said, "Flee sexual immorality. Every sin that a man does is outside the body, but he who commits sexual immorality sins against his own body. Or do you not know that your body is the temple of the Holy Spirit who is in you, whom you have from God, and you are not your own? For you were bought at a price; therefore glorify God in your body and in your spirit, which are God's" (1 Cor. 6:18–20).

There are four things Paul lays out in this passage. There is an admonition: the faithful must flee from sexual immorality. There is an addition: sexual sin directly alters our lives. There is an admission: we are not our own. And finally, there is an ambition: we are therefore to glorify God in our bodies.

ADMONITION

Notice the force and urgency of Paul's exhortation, his admonition. He states very plainly, "Flee sexual immorality."

Don't misunderstand what he is saying here. He is not saying to flee sex. Some people think to even mention the word is ugly and naughty. On the contrary, within the marriage relationship sex is beautiful, pure, and good. The Bible is absolutely clear on this point. It is a magnificent and joyous experience when placed within the boundaries God affords. Only when we wrench sex out of its God-ordained parameters does it become evil, perverted, and divisive.

For the Christian the issue is not sex per se. It is sex outside God's design. The apostle does not say, "Flee sex"; he says, "Flee sexual immorality." Christians are not antisex. We simply have a higher view of it than mere animal instinct.

The real issue here is immorality. The Greek word for "immorality" is *porneia*, the same root from which we get the word *pornography*. *Porneia* appears a dozen times in the New Testament, and in each instance it refers to illicit sexual encounters outside a husband-wife relationship. Sometimes that illicit activity is fornication. Sometimes it is adultery. Sometimes it is homosexuality. Interestingly, no distinction is made among these perversions—

one is not somehow worse than another. Any illicit sexual activity outside the sacred marital bed of a husband and wife is a perversion of God's perfect plan and providence.

Therefore the apostle asserts that whenever temptations in this arena present themselves, we are to flee. In the original Greek text, there is a present imperative in this admonition. It means we shouldn't weigh our options or consider alternatives. In the face of sexual temptation, we are to flee. Literally, we are to run rapidly away—without hesitation, without consideration, without consultation. We are simply to flee. The same word is used in Matthew's account of the infancy of Christ when Mary and Joseph took the baby and fled down to Egypt. They ran away when Herod decreed that all the babies in Bethlehem two years of age and younger would be killed. The same word is found later when Christ's followers ran away in fear following His arrest: "All the disciples forsook Him and fled" (Matt. 26:56). In its every occurrence, the word means immediate departure, flight, a quick escape.

So Paul's admonition is not simply to avoid sexual sin. We are to consciously, purposely, and perpetually run away from it. Get away. Run. Flee. Don't even get in a situation where sexual impropriety is possible. Flee.

Some of us try to fight this kind of temptation. We try to resist it thinking, *Oh, I'm strong. I can handle this situation. I've never fallen yet. I can fight these temptations.* To this, the apostle Paul simply says, "Let him who thinks he stands take heed lest he fall" (1 Cor. 10:12).

He doesn't say, "*Fight* sexual immorality." Nor does he say, "Muster your faith in the face of sexual temptation." We might think, *Well, I'm a Christian; I know the Bible; I've lived a life of faith. I'll just exercise my faith here.*

Sadly, I've watched several friends in the ministry stumble into sexual immorality, and I've seen the catastrophic results in both their personal and professional lives. Invariably, they were men who thought they had the faith to avoid such a moral earthquake.

That is why Paul is entirely unambiguous here. He does not say to "faith it." His admonition is crystal clear: "Flee sexual immorality." Get out of there. Run. Don't hesitate. Don't weigh the situation. Don't stop to consider your options. Don't even pause to pray about it. Just get out of there. Flee.

Now when temptations come in the realm of the spirit, that is when we are supposed to use faith. (Read Ephesians.) That's when we faith it. When temptations come in the realm of the soul, that is when we fight it. But when temptations come in the realm of the flesh, we are not to muster our faith or fight the good fight. We are supposed to flee. When you feel the temptations of the flesh, get out of there!

ADDITION

The reason we are to flee is simple: sexual immorality brings devastation to all three types of relationships in life—with others, with ourselves, and with God. Sexual immorality affects your worth, your witness, and your worship. It adds an unnecessary dimension of tragedy and destruction to our lives.

Men and women often have different reasons for engaging in illicit sexuality. By and large, women give sex to get love. Many young ladies have never known a father's love. Their souls cry out for someone to love them. So they give their bodies away looking for love.

Men do the opposite. They give love to get sex. To satisfy themselves, they say, "I love you." Yet what they are often saying is, "I love me," and consequently, "I want you to satisfy me." It just comes out "I love you."

Tragically, many teenagers have never witnessed the loving relationship of a husband and wife. They have never seen first-hand a marriage that defies worldly logic. They have never seen a man love his wife like Christ loved the church, nor known a woman willing to love and submit to her husband. The end result is that both men and women feel brutally betrayed and utterly unsatisfied in their most intimate relations.

All too often the church is quick to say, "Don't do it. Just say no. Flee sexual immorality," yet we neglect to tell kids and adults *why* they should abstain from sex until marriage. Well, the apostle Paul was not that inconsistent. He said, "Every sin that a man does is outside the body, but he who commits sexual immorality sins against his own body" (v. 18).

Sexual sin is unlike other sins because it adds consequences to life that other sins don't. Sexual sin marks us and masters us. This type of sin defines us and dominates us. It takes over our minds.

Other kinds of sin make us unclean externally, but sexual sin pollutes us internally. It adds a dimension of destructiveness to our lives—and thus inevitably heralds moral earthquakes like no other sins possibly could.

ADMISSION

The apostle Paul does not stop with an admonition and an addition. He next proffers an admission: "Do you not know that your body is the temple of the Holy Spirit who is in you, whom you have from God, and you are not your own? For you were brought at a price" (vv. 19–20).

In the New Testament, there are two different words that we translate "temple." The first refers to the entire temple complex in Jerusalem—the temple mount, the court of the Gentiles, Solomon's portico, the colonnades, and all the inner courts. The other word is used exclusively for the sacred space just behind the altar and beyond the veil in the inner court—the Holy of Holies.

When Paul says, "Your body is the temple," he uses that second word. He asserts that a believer's body is the most holy place, the dwelling place of the Holy Spirit. It is God's Holy of Holies.

In the Old Testament, God came to the temple and dwelt in that holy place. The *shakinah* glory of God inhabited that space between the cherubim over the mercy seat of the ark in the Holy of Holies. Now, in this dispensation, He says that the believer's body is that sacred place.

Even if we should ever become involved in illicit sexual sin, most of us would never think of committing it in a holy place. We would never think of desecrating a church, for instance. We would never flaunt our brazenness so profligately. Nor would we ever think of going into a beautiful cathedral or a great sanctuary in Bethlehem and committing sexual sin there. In a much more vivid and biblical way, we should recoil at the thought of committing such sin at all, regardless of the place or the geography. God doesn't inhabit a building or a plot of ground or a historic site. He inhabits His temple, and the believer's body is that temple.

We shouldn't anymore think about sexual sin outside the parameters of God's Word in our body than we would in any holy place. Our bodies are, in fact, the only genuinely holy places in the created order.

The truth is, our bodies are not our own, and we have no right to injure property that does not belong to us. God bought us with a price. We were purchased out of the slavemarket of sin by Jesus Christ Himself—at great price. "In Him we have redemption through His blood, the forgiveness of sins, according to the riches of His grace" (Eph. 1:7).

AMBITION

Finally, the apostle Paul portrays an appropriate ambition for our lives: "Therefore, glorify God in your body and in your spirit, which are God's" (v. 20).

What should be our ambition in life? Should it be to satisfy our own personal whims, our own personal desires, our own personal expectations? Or should it be to glorify Jesus Christ?

Paul makes the case clearly: We ought to glorify God in all that we are and all that we do. He states this mandate in the strongest possible language. This sentence is even cast in the imperative mood. This is not an option for the believer. We are to radiate the life of Christ and His ownership of us with our whole being—including our bodies. In every way, in every matter, in every manner, we are to glorify God.

Yet how can we glorify God in our bodies? When we come face-to-face with temptation, there are three questions we should ask. When I was seventeen years old, I wrote these three questions in the flyleaf of my Bible. I've written them in every Bible I've owned since.

The first question is "Can I thank God for it?" The Bible says, "In everything give thanks; for this is the will of God in Christ Jesus for you" (1 Thess. 5:18). At every temptation, I ask myself, "If I go ahead and do this, can I look back after it's done and thank God for it?" If not, then I need to flee. I need to get out of there.

The second question is this: "Can I do it in Jesus' name?" The Bible says, "Whatever you do in word or deed, do all in the name of the Lord Jesus" (Col. 3:17). I ask myself, "If I go ahead and do this, will I actually be able to do it in Jesus' name." If not, then I need to flee. I need to get out of there.

The third and final question is "Can I do it for God's glory?" The Bible says, "Therefore whether you eat or drink, or whatever you do, do it all to the glory of God" (1 Cor. 10:31). I ask myself, "Can I possibly do this for God's glory?" If not, then I need to flee. I need to get out of there.

God calls us to purity of mind, morals, motives, and marriages. Paul's words of admonition, addition, admission, and ambition offer us a glorious hope—and a way to avoid the devastation of the innumerable moral earthquakes of our time.

Moral Soundings
• Have you ever faced sexual temptation and tried to fight, resist, or muster faith against it? • Have you therefore made victory over sexual temptation practically impossible? • Have you ever consciously fled from temptation? • Have you ever fully made the admission that you are not your own? • Can you honestly say that in all of your relationships God receives the glory He is due?

–6–

MORAL INTERSECTIONS

Thy word is a lamp unto my feet
and a light unto my path.
Psalm 119:105, KJV

The earthquake that struck the San Francisco Bay area in 1989 collapsed a section of the freeway which connects the cities of Oakland and San Francisco—including a long span of double-decked viaduct. The results were horrifying. Not only were hundreds of motorists injured and stranded in the immediate aftermath of the quake, but precarious driving conditions continued in the region for weeks and months afterward. Even after the rubble had been removed, the weakened bridges demolished, and the damaged pavement barricaded, hazards abounded for drivers.

Just imagine: the entire roadway system was altered overnight. Streets ceased to be passable; traffic light operations, rush-hour flow patterns, and contraflow schemes were all disrupted; one-way streets suddenly had to accommodate two- way traffic; and residential streets became primary arteries. Detours became the norm rather than the exception. Wrong turns were common occurrences.

Most motorists, even given the best of driving conditions, have made the mistake of turning the wrong way down a one-way street. It is such an easy mistake to make. When confused by an unfamiliar setting, pressured by the flow of traffic, and panicked by indecision, anyone can take that wrong turn. We momentarily lack discernment and direction; therefore, we inevitably make mistakes.

Life has unexpected twists, turns, and intersections as well. Though they come at different times for each of us, they are strikingly similar—each involves a moral decision we must make. At every intersection we must decide which way to go, and a wrong turn at a moral intersection of life can affect our journey for a lot of miles. Some people who make a wrong turn at a moral intersection spend years of their lives getting nowhere on side streets, cul-de-sacs, and dead ends. Others end up having wrecks that cause hurt and damage to others. At these moral intersections of life, the question isn't whether to turn right or left; the question is whether to turn *right* or *wrong*.

It's frightening to think of turning loose a fifteen- or sixteen-year-old girl or boy to drive in a major metropolitan area, but it is something that most parents must face at one time or another. As a father, I was determined to teach my girls at least five basic lessons about driving.

The first was read your map and know the directions to your destination ahead of time. In other words, I didn't want them to get to a major intersection and not know which way to turn. At one point, we lived fifteen miles from the Christian school they attended. When it came time for them to drive, I didn't want them to travel all the way across our tangled metropolitan area only to get to an intersection and not know which way to turn. I wanted them to read the map ahead of time, so that they would know which way to turn.

The second lesson I taught them was stop when you see a red light. Now, that sounds pretty simplistic, but simple rules are generally the best rules. Besides, it is absolutely amazing how many motorists ignore this common sense dictum.

The third lesson I taught my girls was yield the right of way to others. There is no need to tempt fate. More importantly, there is no need to tempt harried commuters in the snarl of city streets either.

The fourth lesson was submit to the proper authorities. Obey all the traffic signs. Obey the police. When we remain under authority, we will inevitably be safer.

The fifth lesson I taught my girls was look both ways before you go. But when you go, really go. Don't hesitate in the middle of an intersection. Look both ways, and when it's clear, go on your way.

Clearly, these five lessons are basic to roadway protocol, but they are equally applicable to all our other everyday affairs—to our moral journeys through this life.

TURNING POINT

Joseph came to a moral intersection of life as a relatively young man. He was forced to take the wheel and drive himself. Up until this time his dad had made many of his decisions for him. Yet when we read about this chapter in his life, we find him in a precarious situation—a moral intersection.

The road that brought him to this particular intersection was filled with all kinds of mountaintops and valleys. He drove on the mountaintop for a while as the favorite son of his father, receiving from him the fabled coat of many colors. Later, he had a dream in which God revealed to him His plan for his life. He knew what God wanted him to do. He was to be the leader of a great nation. So Joseph cruised along with the top down, enjoying the beautiful view as he drove over the mountaintop. Suddenly his journey took him down into the valley.

Because of the jealousy and hatred of his brothers, Joseph was thrown into a pit and later sold. His slavery to the Ishmaelites took him down into Egypt. His journey descended even farther into the valley. He was sold on a block and purchased by a man named Potiphar who made him his personal slave—a servant in his home.

Eventually Joseph's character and integrity caused him to be made ruler over all of Potiphar's home. He was young, bright, intelligent, and powerful. He was riding high again, but it was not to last. Shortly thereafter, he arrived at a great moral intersection:

It came to pass after these things that his master's wife cast longing eyes on Joseph, and she said, "Lie with me." But he refused and said to his master's wife, "Look, my master does not know what is with me in the house, and he has committed all that he has to my hand. There is no one greater in this house than I, nor has he kept back anything from me, but you, because you are his wife. How then can I do this great wickedness, and sin against God?" So it was, as she spoke to Joseph day by day, that he did not heed her, to lie with her or to be with her." (Gen. 39:7–10)

Notice, Joseph not only resisted her seductions; he didn't even want to be in the same vicinity as his mistress.

"But it happened about this time, when Joseph went into the house to do his work, and none of the men of the house was inside, that she caught him by the garment, saying, 'Lie with me.' But he left his garment in her hand, and fled and ran outside" (Gen. 39:11–12). He got out of there as fast as he possibly could. She ripped the very shirt off his back. Then, to cover her own sin, she said he had tried to rape her. She falsely accused him. As a result of this accusation, Potiphar had him thrown into an Egyptian dungeon. Joseph came to another moral intersection. Amazingly, he put into practice those same five principles I taught my daughters when they were first learning to drive.

READ THE MAP

Read the map and know your directions beforehand. When I taught my daughters to drive, I wanted them to think ahead, to know which way they were going to turn when they arrived at any given intersection. The reason is simple: If we are driving along in the far right lane and suddenly find ourselves at an intersection where we need to make an immediate left, we will need to maneuver through three or four lanes of on-rushing traffic to make the correct turn. We thus get into all kinds of problems and confusion. We bring confusion to others. We may even have a wreck. Sometimes we make wrong turns and are then loathe to ask for help. What is it about us that when we get lost or we make a wrong turn, we just won't ask anybody for directions? How many times has that kind of scenario been repeated in our lives?

Notice Joseph: He had already decided which way he was going to turn before he got to that moral intersection. Years before, God gave him a dream. God revealed to him that He was going to use him in a mighty way. Joseph made some decisions in his own heart, and in his own life. As a result, the Bible tells us that "the Lord was with Joseph" (Gen. 39:2). That is why he became successful.

Joseph made the right turn at that intersection of life because he had already decided—he knew the route, and he had determined which way he was going to turn before he even got there. Like Daniel would years later, he purposed in his heart that he would not defile himself. Joseph didn't stand in the intersection of Mrs. Potiphar's passion, ring his hands, and say, "Well, what should I do? Should I, or should I not?" He'd already made up his mind, before he ever got to that intersection. Unfortunately, many of us make wrong turns in life because we wait until we get into the middle of the intersection before we decide what we're going to do.

Remember Samson? He made some wrong turns early in life. The rest of his life was spent on side streets, cul-de-sacs, and dead ends. Interestingly, Samson and Joseph had a lot in common. But what made the difference between these two young men was that when they came to moral intersections in life, one turned the right way and one turned the wrong way. But why? They both were blessed with striking personalities and good looks. In fact, the narrative says Joseph was handsome in form and appearance, and we know Samson was strapping, virile, athletic, and comely.

We read of both of them that "the Lord was with them." They both found themselves away from home in the midst of ungodly people—Samson amidst the Philistines, Joseph with the Egyptians—living in hostile environments. They even faced similar temptations—immoral relations with powerful, persistent, tempestuously seductive women.

Yet in nearly identical circumstances, we find that one turned right at that intersection and one turned wrong. Why? What was the difference?

As we said before, Joseph had already decided which way he was going to turn before he got there. Samson hadn't. He got in the middle of the intersection with Delilah, and she kept coming back. He didn't know what he was going to do, so he didn't do anything for a while. He was indecisive. He stood there for a time until finally he allowed his flesh to direct his way. He made a last-second turn—in the wrong direction.

Joseph's decision, on the other hand, is the kind of common sense resolve all of us need to exercise. Make a promise to God, to yourself, to your parents, to your future husband, to your future wife, or to your future children. Draw a line, and set your mind to it. Draw a line in your heart and your mind, and don't cross it. Then some Friday night when you get out into that moral intersection and see your friends turning the wrong way, you will know what you are going to do long before you even get there. You won't need to panic or freeze in indecision. You will have already decided the right turn.

That was one of the secrets of Joseph's life. Read the map, and know the directions beforehand.

JUST SAY NO

The second lesson Joseph applied was *stop when you see a red light.* "[Potiphar's] wife cast longing eyes on Joseph, and she said, 'Lie with me.' But he refused" (Gen. 39:7–8).

Stop when you see a red light. What an important lesson. How many people have been hurt because somebody was in such a big hurry that they ran through a red light? They thought they wouldn't get caught. They thought no police were around. They thought they could get by with it.

It is dangerous to run a red light, especially at moral intersections. Joseph was an overcomer because he said no from the start. The first time Potiphar's wife came to him he didn't flirt with her, think it was cute, or say, "Well, I'll never get into this, but I'll just play around with it awhile and see how far she takes it." No, he said no from the very beginning. He refused. When he saw that red light flashing he stopped.

One of the most important words in any language is *no*. Joseph knew that. As a result, he refused. He was able to stand firm because he was unwavering from the start. That little two-letter word is the secret to overcoming many of the temptations we face in this life.

Now don't think Joseph wasn't tempted here. He was away from home in a foreign country, lonely, and with little to lose. He had no family there to embarrass or a reputation to maintain or defend; nobody knew him. He was also young and handsome. Potiphar's wife was a woman of power and undoubtedly a woman of beauty. Her seductions certainly would have appealed to his pride and fed his ego. It seemed like everybody else in the culture around him was already turning at similar moral intersections. He should have been flattered, many of his peers would have told him. But he knew how to say an important word—*no*. Why? Because he had already decided which way he was going to turn before he got there, and he stopped when he saw a red light.

But Potiphar's wife wouldn't take no for an answer. She came back day after day. Still, Joseph did not heed her. He didn't even want to be near her. He stayed out of her vicinity.

Some of us are foolish enough to think that we can flirt with sensual desires, that we can joke and kid about them, without actually being affected by them. For instance, think about what our kids are watching on television these days. We might say, "Oh, we don't have cable. We don't have HBO or MTV or anything like that." But, what about ABC, NBC, CBS, and FOX?

During one recent episode of "Roseanne," a highly-rated network program, the star successively dealt with her homosexual business partner who had fallen in love with a delivery man, her daughter's sexual exploits with her live-in lover, and the dilemma of her twelve-year-old son who kept mysteriously disappearing. When Roseanne sent her daughter to spy on the boy, she came back with the horrifying news, "Mom, it's worse than you ever thought. He's been going to a church!" It appears that only morality is unconscionable these days.

An episode of "NYPD Blue," another top-ranked network program, had full-length nude shower scenes and was filled with sexual innuendoes and euphemisms. On "Sisters," yet another network sitcom, Norma decided to have a child with her lesbian lover while Georgie's psychiatrist urged her to fantasize about somebody else's husband. "Friends" features a cast of several very attractive and witty single adults who sit around discussing the weirdest places where they've indulged in sexual immorality. On one episode, the characters took the Lord's name in vain over a dozen times in one thirty-minute show. "Frasier," still another popular network program, found humor one week in the fact that the main character arranged a blind date for his new boss and his father's physical therapist, only to find out that the boss is a homosexual and interpreted the occasion as a date with Frasier. In another episode, Frasier fondly recalled how his dad bought him a prostitute for his sixteenth birthday—and all the other "joys" of illicit teenage sex. All of these shows are popular primetime network broadcast programs.

How would Joseph have responded at that moral intersection if every night for hours on end that's what he'd been filling his mind with? Do we wonder at the explosion of teenage sexual sin today?

Sadly, statistics indicate that Christian kids are about as involved in immorality as the other kids are.

Joseph was able to resist temptation because he took a strong stand from the very first. He knew which way he was going to turn. When he saw a red light, he stopped and said no.

YIELD THE RIGHT OF WAY

There is a third lesson Joseph learned: *yield the right-of-way to others*. Certainly, that is an important lesson when we are learning to drive. Have respect for the other drivers. Be considerate to those around you. Give way to them. Yield to those who have the right-of-way.

At Joseph's moral intersection he showed respect for three people: first for Potiphar, second for himself, and finally for Potiphar's wife.

"Look," he said, "My master does not know what is with me in the house, and he's committed all that he has in my hands." Joseph respected Potiphar. He respected his position as a husband. He considered how Potiphar would feel if he found out that his trusted servant had carried on an affair with his wife. He valued Potiphar's friendship. As a result, he refused to steal the affection that was due Potiphar from his own wife. Joseph yielded to others.

He also respected himself. "There's no one greater in this house," he asserted, "nor has he kept back anything from me." Joseph had too much respect for the integrity of his faith and commitment to the Lord to defile his body in an adulterous, illicit affair. He had too much self-respect to indulge in that kind of perversity. One of the things that we jettison when we make wrong turns at moral intersections is self-respect. Joseph simply had too much regard for what God had confirmed and established in his life to yield to temptation in that sordid fashion.

Finally, Joseph demonstrated respect for Potiphar's wife. He respected her enough to say no to her advances. He said no because "you are his wife." He was able to clearly distinguish the difference between lust and love. Lust often comes disguised as love, but it is just a disguise. Love has the other person's highest ideal in mind. Joseph knew that, so he said no.

SUBMIT TO AUTHORITY

The fourth lesson Joseph learned was *submit to the proper authorities.* That is what I tried to teach my daughters when they were first learning to drive. They were to obey the law. I told them that when they saw a traffic sign, they were to obey it. They were to submit to the proper authorities. If they were, by chance, stopped by a policeman, they were to show him respect and submit to him as an authority that God ordained and appointed over us.

Notice how Joseph followed this basic mandate: "How then can I do this great wickedness, and sin against God?" he asked. He recognized that, ultimately, all sin is rebellion against God. All breaches of conduct are an affront to His authority in our lives. All moral lapses are slights against Him—and Him only.

In the final analysis, it is our love for God that keeps us from turning the wrong way at the moral intersections of life. When we find ourselves in a situation where we are unlikely to get caught, where no one will know, often it is only our relationship with the Lord Jesus Christ that can keep us from turning the wrong way. This is the one thing that can keep us pure.

Does the fact that our involvement with sin is an affront against God ever come to our mind? Why not? Is it because we have persistently refused to nurture a conscious awareness that He is always with us? Joseph was certainly aware of this danger. Thus, throughout this text we find that "the Lord was with him."

Why don't some of us have a conscious awareness of God's presence with us? Perhaps it is because we constantly fill our minds with sensuality from television, movies, and music—and seldom with the Word of God. One of Joseph's secrets was he lived a life conscious of the awareness God.

LOOK BOTH WAYS

Joseph's final lesson was *look both ways and then go*. I taught my daughters: When you get to the intersection, look both ways; then, if the coast is clear, don't hesitate out there—go on through the intersection. Notice that Joseph didn't try to fight his temptation. He fled it. He got out of there. Potiphar's wife ran up, grabbed him, and said, "Lie with me." But Joseph left his garment in her hand and ran out the door. He lost his coat, but he kept his character. He lost his vest, but he kept his virginity. He looked both ways, and he got out of there. Look both ways, and go.

The Bible says, "No temptation has overtaken you except such as is common to man; but God is faithful, who will not allow you to be tempted beyond what you are able, but with the temptation will also make an escape, that you may be able to bear it" (1 Cor. 10:13). Moral intersections in life are inevitable. We all get there sooner or later. The only question is, which way are we going to turn? If we learn from Joseph and apply these principles to our own lives, then what was said of him might be said of us, "The Lord was with Joseph, and he was a successful man" (Gen. 39:2).

Moral Soundings

- Have you decided which way you will turn?
- What is the map you've consulted to chart your way?
- Have you already fallen into the pattern of sin?
- What can you do to break that pattern?
- Are there any common sense steps toward victory that you may have neglected?

THE HIGH COST OF LOW LIFE

A man cannot be established through wickedness,
but the righteous cannot be uprooted.
Proverbs 12:3, NIV

Necessity is the mother of invention—but desperation is the author of breakthroughs.

We have all seen how productive we can be—when we absolutely have to. When our lives or well being—or those of our loved ones—are at stake, we can accomplish marvels. When we have exhausted all other resources, we will do whatever is necessary to achieve our desired ends.

That certainly was the case with Captain Naaman. He was the commander in chief of the king's armies in ancient Syria—a man mighty in valor. But Naaman had leprosy. He was about to leave his job and his family to live out his days in a leper colony. He had a little servant girl in his home that had been taken as a captive in a raid over in Samaria. This servant said to Naaman's wife, "If only my master were with the prophet who is in Samaria! He would heal him of his leprosy" (2 Kings 5:3).

Having exhausted every other means of healing, Naaman set out with a letter of introduction from the king and some money to seek his cure. First though, he went to an earthly prince instead of the prophet of God. He tried to buy his cure by offering money. He thought he could be cured with what he had. Naaman then thought he could be cured with whom he knew. He took the letter from the king and presented it to the prince; but of course, it was all to no avail. Once again suffering disappointment, Naaman finally learned that he just needed to do what he had originally been told.

He inquired of the prophet, Elisha, who then sent word by his servant Gehazi, "Go and wash in the Jordan seven times, and . . . you shall be clean" (2 Kings 5:10). Naaman went away in a rage of fury. He was too proud to do that: "Are not the Abanah and the Phapar, the rivers of Damascus, better than all the waters of Israel?" (2 Kings 5:12).

Fortunately, one of his servants said, "My father, if the prophet had told you to do something great, would you not have done it. How much more then, when he says to you, 'Wash, and be clean'?" (2 Kings 5:13).

Then the proud, heroic conqueror Naaman went down to the Jordan, took off his regal, royal robes, and submerged himself seven times. The Bible tells us that his skin became like that of a little child. Then Naaman and all his servants went back to the man of God. He stood before Elisha and said, "Now I know that there is no God in all the earth, except in Israel; now therefore, please take a gift from your servant" (2 Kings 5:15).

The prophet answered, "As the Lord lives, before whom I stand, I will receive nothing" (2 Kings 5:16). Even though Naaman urged him, he still refused. Elisha the prophet didn't want Naaman to think salvation was something that could be bought. It was a free gift.

So, Naaman responded:

> If you will not, please let me, your servant be given as much earth as a pair of mules can carry, for your servant will never again make burnt offerings and sacrifices to any other god but the Lord. But may the Lord forgive your servant for this one thing: When my master enters the temple in Rimmon to bow down and he is leaning on my arm and I bow there also—when I bow down in the temple of Rimmon, may the Lord forgive your servant for this. (2 Kings 5:17–18, NIV)

Elisha told him to go in peace and sent him on his way. But after Naaman left, Gehazi, Elisha's servant, said to himself, "My master was too easy on Naaman, this Aramean, by not accepting from him what he brought. As surely as the Lord lives, I will run after him and get something from him" (2 Kings 5:20, NIV).

So Gehazi caught up with Naaman's group. Naaman saw him and came down from the chariot to meet him. "'Is everything all right?' he asked. 'Everything is all right,' Gehazi answered" (2 Kings 5:21, NIV). But of course, it wasn't—at least, not quite: "My master sent me to say, 'two young men from the company of the prophets have just come to me from the hill company of Ephraim. Please give them a talent of silver and two sets of clothing'" (2 Kings 5:22, NIV). This was an out-and-out lie.

"By all means take two talents," said Naaman. He urged Gehazi to accept them, and then tied up the two talents of silver in two bags, with two sets of clothing. He gave them to two of his servants, and they carried them ahead of Gehazi. When Gehazi came to the hill, he took the things from the servants and put them away in the house. [He hid them.] He sent the men away and they left. Then he went in and stood before his master Elisha.

"Where have you been, Gehazi?" Elisha asked.

"Your servant didn't go anywhere," Gehazi answered. [Another lie.]

But Elisha said to him, "Was not my spirit with you when the man got down from the chariot to meet you? Is this the time to take money, or to accept clothes, olive groves, vineyards, flocks, herds, or menservants and maidservants? Naaman's leprosy will cling to you and to your descendants forever." Then Gehazi went from Elisha's presence and he was leprous, as white as snow. (2 Kings 5:23–27, NIV)

GRACE AND JUDGMENT

In this long narrative story from Scripture we see the wonderful, marvelous cure of Naaman at the Word of the living God. We see how his cure was freely given—as wonderfully free as Gehazi's judgment was horribly deserved. One can hardly believe that in one chapter of Scripture we descend from such heavenly heights to such dastardly depths.

Yet, both grace and judgment are essential elements of the same gospel message. They always have been. They always will be.

It all started in the Garden. Adam and Eve impoverished themselves amidst the riches of Eden by sinning against God and transgressing His Word. Suddenly in the shadow of plenty, they knew real lack. They became utterly destitute.

Pain and sorrow became their lot (see Gen. 3:16). Hardship and calamity became the course of their lives (see Gen. 3:17). They fell from riches to rags, from the watered garden to the wretched wasteland (see Gen. 3:18–19, 23–24).

When God came to them in the cool of the day, they were huddled together in their misery and their shame (see Gen. 3:7–8). He looked upon their broken estate and saw their pitiful poverty.

So how did He respond to them? What did God do?

First, He pronounced a word of judgment on them. He conducted a kind of courtroom lawsuit against them: questioning, interrogating, cross-examining, and sentencing. He judged their sin (see Gen. 3:14–19).

Next, He pronounced a word of hope for them. He opened the prophetic scrolls and revealed the promise of a Deliverer, a Savior. He gave them good news (see Gen. 3:15).

And, finally, He confirmed His Word with deeds. He clothed them in the hide of an animal. He covered them. He showed them mercy. He matched His righteous judgment with grace and charity (see Gen. 3:21).

There in the cool of the garden, God confronted the sin of Adam and Eve, and He did it by meeting their deprivation with judgment first and gracious good news immediately after.

This is the biblical model, the divine model, of the gospel. It announces to sinful men that they have disobeyed a holy God, that He will find them out, and that He will pronounce judgment against them. But it also offers hope. It tells sinful men that there is a Savior who crushes the serpent's head and redeems them from their plight.

The gospel always adheres to this pattern. It involves two clear messages: the coming judgment of God, and God's generous way of escape in Christ the sin-bearer.

Thus, we can see this evangelical pattern in the testimony of the prophet Isaiah. First, he announced judgment; then, he announced a way of escape. He said:

> Cry loudly, do not hold back; raise your voice like a trumpet, and declare to My people their transgression, and to the house of Jacob their sins. . . . Is this not the fast which I choose, to loosen the bonds of wickedness, to undo the bands of the yoke, and to let the oppressed go free, and break every yoke? Is it not to divide your bread with the hungry, and bring the homeless poor into the house; when you see the naked, and to cover him; and not to hide yourself from your own flesh? Then your light will break out like the dawn, and your recovery will speedily spring forth; and your righteousness will go before you; the glory of the LORD will be your rear guard. Then you will call, and the LORD will answer; you will cry and He will say, "Here I am." If you remove the yoke from your midst, the pointing of the finger, and speaking wickedness, and if you give yourself to the hungry, and satisfy the desire of the afflicted, then your light will rise in darkness, and your gloom will become like midday. And the LORD will continually guide you, and satisfy your desire in scorched places, and give strength to your bones; and you will be like a watered garden, and like a spring of water whose waters do not fail. And those from among you will rebuild the ancient ruins; you will raise up the age-old foundations; and you will be called the repairer of the breach, the restorer of the streets in which to dwell. (Isa. 58:1, 6–12, NASB)

God made His evangelistic program clear to Isaiah. First, he was to tell the people of Judah that they were in sin: "Declare to my people their transgression." But then, he was to reveal the way out. They were to fast in repentance—but, they were not to starve themselves in a ritual fast, but to loosen the bonds of wickedness, to let the oppressed go free, to feed the hungry, to invite the homeless into their homes, to provide clothing for the naked. Grace was to abound.

First, he announced wrath against sin; second, he announced grace covering over sin and charity soothing the hurts of sin.

Jesus, too, confirmed this pattern of gospel proclamation. When He began His public ministry in the town of Nazareth, He went into the synagogue, as was His custom, and stood up to read. What He read was significant: the passage from Isaiah that deals with the coming of the Messiah.

Who is the Messiah? The Anointed One who preaches the gospel to the poor:

> *"The Spirit of the LORD is upon Me,*
> *Because He has anointed Me*
> *To preach the gospel to the poor;*
> *He has sent Me to heal the brokenhearted,*
> *To proclaim liberty to the captives*
> *And recovery of sight to the blind,*
> *To set at liberty those who are oppressed;*
> *To proclaim the acceptable year of the LORD." (Luke 4:18–19)*

Isaiah had prophesied that the Anointed One would go into the highways and byways to heal the lame, to give sight to the blind, and to comfort the brokenhearted. Jesus demonstrated His messianic office by doing literally what Isaiah said He would do. So in the synagogue He boldly announced the prophetic fulfillment: "Today this Scripture is fulfilled in your hearing" (Luke 4:21).

Christ never shied away from announcing God's condemnation of sin (Matt. 7:13–23). But neither did He hesitate to announce the good news of hope (Matt. 11:28–30).

Jesus proved He was the Messiah by wedding grace and judgment. He authenticated His claims by modeling the whole gospel in both word and deed.

GEHAZI'S MISTAKE

The Bible says, "The heart is deceitful above all things" (Jer. 17:9). The truth is, one of the most dangerous times in the life of a believer is right after a great victory. Whether we've just knocked down the walls of Jericho or won a spiritual battle over sin, afterwards, we tend to put our trust in our past achievements. When we become self-confident and proud, we begin to overrate our ability to deal with situations; and if we can deal with situations on our own, we have no need for prayer. God doesn't have to help us in order for victory to be assured. How quickly we forget our true Source of victory. That sinful forgetfulness has ever been the problem of God's people.

God commanded parents to instruct their children in the way of the Lord (Deut. 6:6–9). Why did He make this command? It was so neither the parents nor the children would forget the mighty acts the Lord had done for Israel. Why was Passover instituted? To help Israel remember God's mercy on their firstborn and His love for them, as well as His terrible punishment on Egypt. Why was Israel constantly being bound into captivity? Israel continually forgot that God saved His people. They would forget, bring in their idols, anger God, and He would bind them into captivity until they remembered His power to save them and repented of their sins. In the New Testament, Christ himself instructs us to observe the Lord's Supper: "Do this in remembrance of me" Luke 22:19; 1 Cor. 11:24). What should we remember? The pure sacrifice of Christ for our sinful souls. If we forget God, His power, and His mighty acts of love for us, we are setting ourselves up. If we forget, we soon believe that we can tackle anything. Our pride begins our fall. If we're not careful, we become prone to prayerlessness. We trust in yesterday's commitment and hope that it will suffice for today.

The apostle Paul tells us, "Let him who thinks he stands take heed lest he fall" (1 Cor. 10:12). That exhortation perfectly describes the precarious position in which our pride places us. A fall is almost certainly inevitable. Our ensuing fall should be a matter of concern—but also of analysis. If we understand why and how we get into a proud position, and consequently fall, we may be able to avoid it later.

There are four principal parts in a fall—all of them vividly illustrated in Gehazi's foolish episode: first, it's cause; second, it's curse; third, it's consequence; and fourth, it's cure. Each part must be analyzed individually to better understand the whole.

SIN'S CAUSE

What causes a man like Gehazi, Elisha's faithful servant—a man who had walked with Elisha, seen miracle after miracle, witnessed God's power, who knew what it was to be around the glory of God—to so easily stumble?

He took four descending steps. First, he saw. He saw Naaman come back to Elisha after he was cured and offer Elisha some money. He then harbored that sight in his mind, which led to the second step.

He coveted. He started to think about the situation. He calculated his potential profits. He began to covet, plan, and plot.

Third, he took. He went after Naaman and told him a pack of lies. He then took the great man's talents of silver and articles of clothing. Yes, he took them!

Fourth, he hid. He put all his contraband away in his own house. He sent the men away, and then he went over to confront Elisha.

Those four steps are terribly predictable. They are the same four steps that everyone who fell in the Bible committed, and they are the same four steps you and I take. What happened in the Garden of Eden? The woman saw the fruit. She saw that it was good—she coveted. Eve then took the forbidden fruit; afterwards, she and Adam hid from God. Similarly, King David was not where he was supposed to be when the time came to go to battle. He was at the palace. One day he looked out on the side of Mount Zion, and there on the rooftop below was a lady bathing. He saw her—

the first step. Then he began to think about what he had seen. He began to harbor the image in his heart. He began to covet. He sent word to find out who she was. Next, he took her and committed adultery. Finally, he tried to cover over his sin by having her husband Uriah, his faithful soldier, slain on the field of battle. He hid.

We're no different. We go through the same process. It is not a sin to be tempted. Sin comes when we don't let something just pass right on through our minds.

THE CURSE

The curse is that these four steps soon set patterns in our lives. One sin leads to another. One sin attempts to cover another. We tell one lie to cover another lie. It is a miserable, vicious cycle. If spouses are unfaithful to their mates, they have to start lying. They have to cover one lie here, one lie there. Teenagers go out and do what their parents have forbidden them to do, and what happens? They have to lie here and lie there. They wonder to whom they told this and to whom they told that and must make sure everyone will collaborate their story. That is the curse of sin. It sets a pattern.

It happens in the work force. When an employee is insubordinate in the place of employment, all too often he or she has to tell lies to cover the breach. Every lie or excuse is followed by another. Soon there are enough lies to construct a fantasy world. The first lie seems small enough, but with each successive lie, the situation expands into a mass of falsity. More lies are told to tie up loose ends which demand more lies and on and on and on. Gehazi discovered that only too quickly.

Naaman asked him if everything was all right. He nonchalantly replied that it was. That was, of course, a lie. The first lie of many. Everything was not all right. Gehazi went on, "My master sent me." That too was a lie, and it was still just the beginning.

When he got back and Elisha asked him where he had been, he responded, "Your servant did not go anywhere." That was yet another lie. On and on the story went.

Most of us have been there. Sin sets a pattern in motion where we have to tell one lie after another and live our lives looking over our shoulders, wondering who is going to find us out. We wonder what we told him and try to remember what we told her so we can keep our stories straight. What a curse!

Gehazi had a demonstration of God's grace fresh on his mind—the healing of Naaman. But apparently he forgot the other essential aspect of the gospel—a confrontation of our sinfulness. As a result, he suffered terrible consequences.

THE CONSEQUENCE

When Gehazi went out from Elisha's presence he was leprous, as white as snow. Was not God's Spirit with Gehazi, seeing all he did? He got what Naaman had been delivered of. This is a frighteningly clear demonstration of the biblical warning, "Do not be deceived, God is not mocked; for whatever a man sows, that he will also reap" (Gal. 6:7).

He had an opportunity to confess and get clean. Elisha went in and asked him, "Where have your been, Gehazi?" But apparently he was either too proud or too greedy to repent. He had forgotten the essence of the Gospel. So he just kept on lying.

Gehazi perverted the message of Christ. Salvation is free, it can't be bought. That's what Naaman learned when he came back to Elisha. That is why Elisha didn't take anything from him. He wanted Naaman to know that his cleansing was free.

In this story we not only see God's mercy, we see His judgment. The same God who demonstrated lavish mercy to Naaman exercised stern discipline on the sin of Gehazi.

THE CURE

Some think God is only a God of love. If He were only a God of love, everyone would go to heaven. If He were only a God of wrath, no one would go, because we've all sinned and fallen short of the glory of God.

Thanks be to God: He is both. He is both gracious, merciful, and long-suffering; *and* He is just, holy, and altogether righteous. Because He is both, He is our cure.

Moral Soundings
• Who are you more like, Naaman or Gehazi? • Are you more prone to neglect the grace or the judgment of God? • Do you find yourself taking the downward steps of sin and temptation? • Are you more enraptured by the cause, the curse, or the consequences of sin than by its cure?

–8–

GOING DOWN

Pride goes before destruction,
and a haughty spirit before a fall.
Proverbs 16:18

In any natural disaster, the greatest heartbreaks and the greatest joys focus on the way people respond to the crisis. Feats of heroism, selflessness, and courage abound in times of need. Simultaneously, the exploitive greed and avarice of men seem to come to the fore in the most tragic of circumstances. The Bay Area earthquake in 1989 highlighted both. Rescuers risked their lives for others hour after hour, day after day in the aftermath of the disaster. At the same time looters were pillaging the remains of victims' homes, shops, and businesses.

While many neighbors shared selflessly, others proved to be appallingly callous. One landlord reportedly continued to charge rent on his Marin apartments even though no one could live in the damaged building. A restaurant owner was charging fifteen dollars for a sandwich the night of the quake. Some people broke into damaged stores and stole as much as they could carry away. These people all saw a chance to profit from the disaster.

It should not surprise us that the same kind of dynamic is at work in the spiritual life. Following a moral earthquake, we are liable to see both the best and the worst in man. We are also likely to see the best and the worst in the church.

All of us know that Christians experience problems relating to one another. Christians have arguments and disagreements with each other. But beyond that, Christians sin against one another continually. We harm one another with our thoughts, words, and deeds. Although there is no escaping the fact that we will always continue to sin, two major differences should exist between us and unbelievers. The first is that our standards for conduct—what is right and wrong—are higher because they are God's standards. The other important difference is that God has given us a way of mending and healing those wrongs perpetrated against each other.

A DIFFERENT PATTERN

God has devised a process through which reconciliation takes place, allowing us a second chance with one another. He has also prescribed the manner in which we are to act when involved in a dispute with a Christian brother or sister. The reconciliation occurs privately between the concerned parties. Gossip, slander, and bitter words—common to disputes in worldly situations—are simply inappropriate, and even disgraceful, when Christians are mending their relationships. Indeed, the typical patterns of worldly avarice are explicitly prohibited from the process.

It is not all right for Christians to drag their problems with each other through the world's arena. God has given us a program in the Word of God of how to deal with these things, and it is not to bring them to the world.

It is not all right for a pastor—or even for a lay leader—to divorce, for instance. It is not an option for the believer. Now to be sure, there are a lot of second marriages that are better than the first one was, but there are none that are as good as the first ones *could* have been. We have a job in this world—where over half the marriages now end in divorce—to build a wall as high and as thick as we can, to keep young people from falling off the cliff. We must let them know what the Bible teaches, and at the same time, keep an ambulance waiting at the bottom of the cliff, full of gas, to bandage up and to bind up the lives of those who have fallen. Then we help them see that there is a land of beginning again. This kind of program of reconciliation requires a good deal of balance.

This truth is evident all throughout the dramatic story of Simon Peter. Always brash and bold, Jesus warned him that "Satan has asked for you, that he might sift you as wheat. But I have prayed for you, that your faith should not fail" (Luke 22:31–32).

That must have seemed to be a needless prayer to the apostle. Peter responded saying, "I am ready to go with You, both to prison and to death" (Luke 22:33). He was absolutely confident in his faith, his reliability, and his constancy. Jesus knew better. He said, "The rooster shall not crow this day before you will deny three times that you know me" (Luke 22:34).

I suppose it is unfortunate that despite all the wonderful things Peter did during his career, when his name is mentioned, the first thing we all think of is this one incident which shows him in his worst light. Then again, perhaps it is because of his dramatic failure that this story gives a vivid warning to all of us of the danger of denying our Lord. It clearly reminds us that no one is immune to the possibility of a calamitous spiritual downfall.

Ask a dozen Christians who their favorite apostle is, and the majority of them will probably say Simon Peter. Perhaps the reason is that he is so intensely human. He's just like we are: impulsive, impetuous, and impossible. When he made mistakes, he made big ones. When he spoke unwisely, he spoke very unwisely.

Clearly, Simon Peter did not expect to deny the Lord. In spite of Christ's clear warning, turning his back on the Lord Jesus Christ was the farthermost thing from Peter's mind. But then, none of us deliberately intend to indulge in a spiritual downfall. None of us actually plan to fall into temptation and sin. Like Peter, we're more inclined to expect that we'll remain forever stalwart. So, we're always a bit shocked when the inevitable happens and we do fall.

It is a very precarious spiritual position to place ourselves in—to assume that we will never fall. It is a dangerous thing to be where Simon Peter was—actually boasting to the Lord, "I am ready to go with You, both to prison and to death." Between that statement of spiritual machismo and his subsequent denial of Christ, Peter obviously underwent a transformation. But again, he certainly did not set out to change. Yet his fall was not sudden or unpredictable. No, his fall was slow, almost an imperceptible alteration within him.

ON THE SLOPES

Almost everyone has heard the term "slippery slope." That phrase refers to some sort of process that occurs so smoothly—many times unwarily—that whoever is on that slope cannot perceive it or does not know how to get off of it. A good example of this is the way an adulterous affair begins.

Most people do not wake up one morning and think, "You know, I think I'm going to begin an affair today." Instead, it begins with a gradual distancing that occurs between a husband and wife—many times in response to some other situations or circumstances occurring in their respective lives. At some point though, the distance becomes so great that they believe it cannot ever be effectively bridged again. True heart separation occurs, and eventually an affair results. This spiritual fall is gradual. It is a process. It takes place in stages, one leading to another in a sort of chain reaction. Once on that slippery slope, we drift ever downward, unable to arrest our inertia. Eventually, our speed carries us farther than we ever thought possible.

Peter's fall was no different. He mistakenly stepped onto that slippery slope. Without realizing it immediately, he followed its downward course. As we look at Peter's life we can discern at least seven steps life that lead him toward his denial.

PRIDE

The first step was pride. Jesus said, "Simon, Simon! Indeed, Satan has asked for you, that he may sift you as wheat. But I prayed for you, that your faith should not fail" (Luke 22:31–32). Jesus warned Peter in the gentlest and most compassionate manner imaginable. So, what was Peter's response? He said, "Lord, I am ready to go with You." It doesn't matter where. If it's prison I'll be with you. I can handle it—whatever *it* might be.

Step one on the spiritual downgrade is thus an overweening confidence in the flesh. It is a dangerous thing to be so sure of ourselves, yet it is almost as if we are intent on training people to flaunt confidence in the flesh by redoubling our efforts to teach self-esteem, self-confidence, self-reliance, and self-actualization.

Moral earthquakes don't just happen. But then, they aren't really plotted and planned either. There isn't a preacher or lay person who has stumbled who really intended to. A great fall comes along in life when we forget that we need to rely on the daily bread of grace, when we begin to rest in the confidence of the flesh. It is all too often fatal when a Christian begins to boast about what he is going to do or not going to do.

The same thing happened to Peter when he stepped out to walk on the water. He was doing fine—until he took his eyes off the Lord and put them on the waves. At that point, he sunk. The fact is, "He who trusts in his own heart is a fool" (Prov. 28:26).

PRAYERLESSNESS

What happens when we exude confidence in the flesh? The answer is that we take the next step on the spiritual downgrade. We resolve ourselves to prayerlessness. Notice the pattern in the life of the disciples: "When He came to the place, He said to them, 'Pray that you may not enter into temptation'" (Luke 22:40).

Well, is that what they did? Not hardly: "When He rose up from prayer, and had come to His disciples, he found them sleeping from sorrow" (Luke 22:45).

Prayerlessness. Pride and self-confidence naturally lead to prayerlessness. They go together, like steak and potatoes, corned beef and cabbage, or peanut butter and jelly. Pride and prayerlessness. One who thinks he can stand alone has no sense of the need for a life of prayer. After all, what need is there to pray if we think ourselves strong enough to resist temptation. For most of us, prayer is an admission of weakness and insufficiency. We know that we can't do what God alone can do. We throw ourselves at His mercy because we realize that our own efforts are woefully inadequate. We pray because we need, and only God can supply the answers to that need.

Sadly though, because Simon Peter was anything but weak and insufficient, because he was unwilling to confess his dire need of God's good and providential work in his life, he abandoned prayer. It was not particularly important to him. He would rather sleep instead. So he did.

Peter's downfall was thus, directly related to his prayerlessness.

PRESUMPTION

The third step along the spiritual downgrade is presumption: "While He was still speaking, [in the garden of Gethsemane] behold, a multitude; and he who was called Judas, one of the twelve, went before them and drew near to Jesus to kiss him. But Jesus said to him, 'Judas, are you betraying the Son of Man with a kiss?' When those around Him saw what was going to happen, they said to Him, 'Lord, shall we strike with a sword?' And one of them struck the servant of the high priest and cut off his right ear" (Luke 22:47–50).

So, who was the mysterious fellow ready to go to war for the cause of Christ? John tells us in his Gospel: "Then Simon Peter having a sword drew it . . . and cut off his right ear" (John 18:10). The reactionary hothead was Simon Peter. What was happening to him?

His problems began with pride. That brought about prayerlessness, and that brought about presumption. It is always an indication of someone being out of touch with the Lord Jesus when we say and do irrational, presumptuous things. A Christian who operates in the energy of the flesh dishonors the name of the Lord and loses the respect of others around him.

Paul thus argued: "I, brethren, do not speak to you as to spiritual people but as to carnal, as to babes in Christ. I fed you with milk and not with solid food; for until now you were not able to receive it and even now you are still not able; for you are still carnal. For where there are envy, strife, and divisions among you, are you not carnal and behaving like mere men?" (1 Cor. 3:1–3).

Operating in the flesh is a real sign of infancy in the Christian life. Simon Peter acted like an undisciplined child when he struck off the ear of that servant.

PARANOIA

The fourth step along the spiritual downgrade is paranoia. Peter exemplified a quintessential paranoia: "Lord, I am ready to go with You, both to prison and to death" (Luke 22:33). That is what he boasted, but the reality was substantially different. "Having arrested Him, they led him into the high priest's house. But Peter followed at a distance" (Luke 22:54).

He wasn't so excited about going to prison with Jesus after all, was he? He followed at a distance. That kind of thing happens all the time. It is the fourth step in this long and tortured chain reaction, from pride to prejudice to presumption to paranoia.

Simon Peter was afraid—of what others might think, of what others might do to him, afraid of his circumstances—a situation we might all be able to identify with. Thus, he was sunk in a sea of fear. It wasn't that he wanted to abandon the faith altogether. He didn't. At least he came to the house of Caiaphas. The rest of Christ's disciples forsook Him and fled in the darkness. No, it wasn't so much that Peter wanted to quit following the Lord. But he followed at a great distance due to his own paranoia. He was gripped with fear.

Jesus said, "No one having put his hand to the plow, and looking back is fit for the kingdom of God" (Luke 9:62). To turn away—even to be distracted—from our calling is a disgrace precisely because it calls into question the authenticity of our faith.

PEER PRESSURE

The fifth step along the downgrade was peer pressure. Notice how Peter yields to the opinions and inclinations of others:

> Peter followed at a distance. Now when they had kindled a fire in the midst of the courtyard and sat down together, Peter sat among them. And a certain servant girl, seeing him as he sat by the fire, looked intently at him and said, "This man was also with Him." But he denied Him, saying, "Woman, I do not know Him." And after a little while another saw him and said, "You also are of them." But Peter said, "Man, I am not." Then after about an hour had passed, another confidently affirmed, saying, "Surely this fellow was also with him, for he is a Galilean." But Peter said, "Man, I do not know what you are saying." (Luke 22:54–60)

What happened? Peer pressure and worldliness finally molded Peter into a member of the crowd. Peter was worried about what other people might think, and as a result, he betrayed his first principles at the drop of a hat. The psalmist says: "Blessed is the man who walks not in the counsel of the ungodly, nor stands in the path of sinners, nor sits in the seat of the scornful" (Ps. 1:1). Sadly, that description hardly fit Peter at this point in his walk.

When Jesus was arrested, He was taken to the house of Caiaphus, and Peter followed. He made some big promises, but now, he was identifying with the world which rejected Jesus. He was sitting among them at the fire denying that he had ever known Him, molded into their world. His sense of identity suddenly shifted from his Master to his peers. He caved in to the expectations of those around him. That, in turn, led to the next downward spiral.

PARALYSIS

The sixth step along the spiritual downgrade is paralysis. Now it appeared, things were going from bad to worse for Simon Peter.

He became more and more insensitive to the Lord. His bold pledge of allegiance just a few hours earlier faded into the background of his consciousness. He became numb to the warning Christ had pronounced concerning the terrible denial—which was now sure to follow. Thus, he arrived at the fire in the courtyard and found that he was spiritually paralyzed.

This always happens when we backslide. The descent is a gradual slippery slope that begins in pride and goes down from there. But, it doesn't go straight down. If we are not careful, in fact, we might even miss its import altogether. We can become so insensitive that we actually, without ever intending it, end up like Peter, denying our Lord.

There is no prayer we need to pray more frequently than the prayer that God will graciously prevent us from getting into a position or a place where we become insensitive to His voice. There is no danger we need to be on guard against any more studiously than spiritual senses dulled to the point that we are frozen from appropriate activity—spiritual or physical.

PERJURY

The final step along the downgrade is perjury. Open denial. Lying. Not once, not twice, but three times Simon Peter lied; and if Simon Peter can do this, which of us can possibly be immune?

Hours before, he had boasted of his willingness to die for the sake of his faith if need be. Now, he is not even willing to be honest in a casual conversation for the sake of his faith. Before, he was a champion of the gospel. Now, he has become a spiritual Casper Milquetoast.

ALL'S WELL THAT ENDS WELL

Thank God this not the conclusion of the story. In the end, Simon Peter marvelously repented and returned to the fold of faithfulness: "And the Lord turned and looked at Peter. Then Peter remembered the word of the Lord, how He had said to him,

'Before the rooster crows, you will deny Me three times.' So Peter went out and wept bitterly" (Luke 22:61–62).

The ultimate result of Peter's tortured walk along the downgrade was the shedding of bitter tears of remorse. He did not remain recalcitrant. He recognized his betrayal for what it was, and God honored that repentance.

Later, when the women came to the tomb following the crucifixion, an angel greeted them and told them, "Go, tell His disciples—and Peter—that He is going before you into Galilee" (Mark 16:7). The message specifically singles out Peter. Jesus especially wanted Peter to know that his one failure didn't make a permanent flop. He was graciously given a second chance.

Still later, the apostle Paul tells us, "[The risen Christ] appeared to Peter, and then to the Twelve" (1 Cor. 15:5, NIV). Somewhere, someplace that day, Christ had a private meeting with Simon Peter. The only way to overcome a spiritual downfall is to rebound into the favor of the Lord. The only recourse is to receive His rest. For Peter, that process began when he wept bitterly—when he cried out in repentance.

There are seven steps to an open denial: pride, prayerlessness, presumption, paranoia, peer pressure, paralysis, and perjury. It all started when Simon Peter began to put his confidence and trust in his own flesh, when he became self-confident, self-assured, and self-actualized.

No wonder the first Beatitude asserts: "Blessed are the poor in spirit" (Matt. 5:3). If we always remain in humble submission to the sovereign purposes of the Lord, many of our sinful problems might never become so great in magnitude. Thus, many a moral earthquake would never occur.

This seven-step descent along the downgrade is, of course, not restricted to Peter alone. It affected many characters throughout the Bible—and it affects us, as well. We must be vigilant against the din of pride in our lives. Yet, even if we fall, God's love does not fall with us; it remains strong, able to lift us again.

God is a God of the second chance. His love for us dictates His actions. He desires to see us reconciled to Him so we may commune with Him and carry out the tasks He has set for us. Therefore, He makes sure that we are reconciled. Christ restored Peter to Himself just as God restores any one of us to His fold. God is the Great Shepherd and loving Father of us all. The God of the second chance delights in that chance being extended and accepted, whether it is to reconcile a sin by one of His children or to cover a multitude of sins when someone is born again. All of Heaven rejoices when either occurs.

Moral Soundings

- Do you find yourself somewhere along the seven step downgrade that leads to a spiritual fall?
- Do you detect the telltale signs of pride, prayerlessness, and presumption in your life?
- What about paranoia, peer pressure, paralysis, or perjury?
- In what ways have you self-confidently relied upon your own flesh?
- Is your spiritual identity tied up with your past spiritual accomplishments—or in Christ?
- Have you arrived at the place of Peter—crying out in repentance?

Part Three:

FROM UNDER THE RUBBLE: HOPE AFTER A FALL

Amazing grace, how sweet the sound,
That saved a wretch like me;
I once was lost but now I'm found,
Was blind but now I see.

—*John Newton*

ॐ

–9–

AND THEN CAME CONVICTION

But David remained at Jerusalem.
2 Samuel 11:1

౭❧

Though the science of seismology has made great strides in the past few years—making the prediction of earthquakes possible from time to time—for the most part, they continue to catch us by surprise. We know what causes them—secret faults—but precision in identifying their timing, location, and intensity, still eludes us. Often they strike when we least expect them.

In October 1989, most Americans, if they were thinking about Northern California at all, were probably thinking about the World Series between the crosstown rival San Francisco Giants and Oakland Athletics. Certainly, they were not thinking about an earthquake. But in less than ten minutes, all that changed. Suddenly the nation was transfixed by the unfolding tragedy that gripped the entire Bay Area.

Moral earthquakes likewise strike when we least expect them. Though the causes of these catastrophes are all too predictable, the moment of devastation is almost always a surprise.

Certainly that was the case with King David in the Old Testament. At the least likely moment, he found himself in the midst of a terrible moral earthquake that would affect him for the rest of his life. And it all happened in the flash of an eye.

The story is sadly familiar:

> In the spring, at the time when kings go off to war, David sent Joab out with the king's men and the whole Israelite army. They destroyed the Ammonites and besieged Rabbah. But David remained in Jerusalem. One evening David got up from his bed and walked around on the roof of the palace. From the roof he saw a woman bathing. The woman was very beautiful, and David sent someone to find out about her. The man said, "Isn't this Bathsheba, the daughter of Eliam and the wife of Uriah the Hittite?" Then David sent messengers to get her. She came to him, and he slept with her. (She had purified herself from her uncleanness.) Then she went back home. The woman conceived and sent word to David, saying, "I am pregnant." So David sent this word to Joab: "Send me Uriah the Hittite." And Joab sent him to David. When Uriah came to him, David asked him how Joab was, how the soldiers were and how the war was going. Then David said to Uriah, "Go down to your house and wash your feet." So Uriah left the palace, and a gift from the king was sent after him. But Uriah slept at the entrance to the palace with all his master's servants and did not go down to his house. When David was told, "Uriah did not go home," he asked him, "Haven't you just come from a distance? Why didn't you go home?" Uriah said to David, "The ark and Israel and Judah are staying in tents, and my master Joab and my lord's men are camped in the open fields. How could I go to my house to eat and drink and lie with my wife? As surely as you live, I will not do such a thing!" Then David said to him, "Stay here one more day, and tomorrow I will send you back." So Uriah remained in Jerusalem that day and the next." (2 Sam. 11:1–12, NIV)

It was the time of year when kings went to battle, but David decided not to go. Instead, he sent Joab, his general, to do his fighting for him. Meanwhile, he stayed in Jerusalem. He was not where he was supposed to be. David should have been out in battle, leading his men. But he stayed behind, in the lap of luxury.

Then one evening, the idle and irresponsible David got up from his bed and walked around on the roof of the palace. From there he spied a woman bathing. The exposed woman was very beautiful, but instead of looking away, as he ought to have, he ogled her. He not only was where he shouldn't have been, now he was looking where he shouldn't have been looking—his second big mistake.

David made the leap from looking to plotting very quickly—as you might well expect—and then came sin.

At this time in his life and career, David had reached the pinnacle of success. He was the undisputed king of Israel. He had driven out the enemies that had so long plagued his people. Not only had he reached the pinnacle of success politically, he had reached the pinnacle of success spiritually as well. He was a man after God's own heart. He had even fulfilled his covenant with Jonathan by showing kindness to Mephiboseth. He had made this crippled son of Jonathan one of his own sons.

It is hard to believe that a man could descend from such heavenly heights to such devilish depths in such a short span of time, but David did. Just as we all do so very often. In fact, the Bible says that all of us have hearts that are "desperately wicked," that are constantly prone to sin, and we are just as likely to embrace perversity at the height of our success as we are in the depths of our despair.

One obvious tactic of the devil is to strike when things are going right—when we are riding the crest of some great victory. He knows that at such times we are apt to be vulnerable—because it is then that we are most likely to let our guard down. Satan knows this only too well.

So, at the moment of his greatest triumph and glory, the beautiful Bathsheba came into David's life. Then came sin.

RECOGNIZE THE CAUSE OF SIN

There is one thing that we all have in common. Though some are rich, some are poor, some are tall, and some are short, all of us have "sinned and fall short of the glory of God" (Rom. 3:23). In fact, "There is none righteous, no not one" (Rom. 3:10).

That is not a fact we generally care to admit. Yet, no one can live in victory until he or she recognizes and realizes the cause of sin. David is a prime example of the cause of sin. If we are honest with God, we will see ourselves in his sad story.

David was out on the roof of his palace. He looked down and happened to see a woman bathing, but he didn't stop there. After all, it is not a sin to let a thought pass through our minds. Sin comes when we don't allow the temptation to pass through. When we begin to harbor it, when we begin to look upon that temptation with intensity, then we get into trouble. David saw. But instead of averting his gaze, he ogled Bathsheba. Then the inevitable happened: he coveted.

You see, he didn't let it go. He saw. He wanted, and then he explored. He sent and inquired about the woman. David, with deliberate premeditation, plotted the parameters and possibilities of his sin. He saw, he coveted, and then he took.

He sent for her, and they committed adultery. Today, we are a bit too sophisticated and cosmopolitan to refer to such breaches as "adultery." We prefer euphemisms for our sin. We don't call people who steal "thieves" anymore. We use a more sophisticated word: we call them "embezzlers." We don't call a person who is addicted to alcohol a "drunkard." Instead, we use the euphemism "alcoholic." Thus we are loathe to call David's sin "adultery." Today we refer to "affairs." Maybe we think that by softening the word, we have softened the sin. We try to gloss over the import and impact of our sinful actions. Nevertheless, the facts can't be avoided. David and Bathsheba didn't simply have an affair, a fling, or a tryst: they committed adultery.

David saw, he coveted, and then he took. Notice the progression. His sin followed the same pattern as every other great moral earthquake in the Bible. When Eve was in the Garden of Eden, she saw; she coveted; and then she took. Following the great battle of Jericho—when the walls came tumbling down—a single Israelite man, Achan, sinned. Because of his violation, a pall fell upon the whole people. It ultimately caused the children of Israel to lose the battle at Ai and lose thirty-six of their men. Predictably, Achan's sin came because first he saw, then he coveted, and finally he took.

REALIZE THE CURSE OF SIN

David found himself in an awful predicament. Bathsheba sent to him and told him she was pregnant. What made this such a difficult situation was that her husband wasn't home and hadn't been home for some time. He had been out fighting David's battle. He was out there on the front lines of the battle—where David should have been. David became frantic—as well he should have. So he called Uriah back from battle and said to him, "Now Uriah, you've been such a great soldier, I appreciate all you have been doing for me. I want to give you a weekend off. You take some rest and relaxation. I want you to go home and relax over the weekend. Then you can go back to battle."

David had a plan. He thought Uriah would go home, go to bed with his wife, and then when he discovered that she was pregnant nobody would ever know that the child she was carrying was conceived in sin.

However, the faithful Uriah would have none of it. He would not cooperate; he was too honorable a man. He went outside the palace by the gate, got out his bedroll, and slept right there. He said, "If all my other friends are out there on the battlefield, why should I come back and go in to the pleasures of my family and my wife. I'm not going to do it. I'm just going to sleep out here."

When David heard Uriah didn't go home he made some plans. He decided to invite the diligent soldier into the palace. David said, "I'm going to get him drunk and then he'll go home to his wife." At this point, it is hard to believe that this is David—the man after God's own heart. But that is the effect of sin: it takes a man and his affections and twists them all out of proportion. So, David got Uriah over to his house and got him drunk. He then shoved him out the door. He nudged him along and said, "Uriah, go on over to your house and see your wife." But Uriah—even in this drunken stupor—stood firm. For the sake of his honor, he refused go.

By this time, David was desperate. So, he sent his loyal servant, Uriah, back to the battle. He also sent word to Joab, the commander in chief, to put Uriah up on the front lines of the battle. This was to be done in such a way that it would be sure to cost the life of Uriah.

That way, David thought, he would be able to adequately cover his heinous sin. No one would need to know that the child Bathsheba was carrying was actually David's. He tried to cover over his sin with treachery, lies, and, finally, the death of Uriah. This is the curse of sin. Once it starts, it takes over; it completely dominates our lives. We find ourselves constantly looking over our shoulders to see if anyone is coming. We have to cover over this sin with a lie. We have to cover over that lie with yet another, and on and on it goes.

After Bathsheba's time of mourning was over, David sent and brought her to his house and she bore him a son, but the thing that David had done was evil in the sight of God. Even if he had been clever enough to hide it from everyone else in the whole world, God knew. David thought that he could sin and win. He thought he could get by with it, but he was wrong.

REVIEW THE CONSEQUENCES OF SIN

David learned all too quickly that the pleasures of sin were but for a season. Nathan the prophet came to him and related a remarkable story of injustice. The story made David mad and he said, "Whoever sins like that ought to restore four-fold." He didn't realize he had just prophesied his own fate. But in fact,

David was soon to discover that it was his household that would suffer fourfold consequences for his sin.

David and Bathsheba had a little boy, but the child perished soon after. The wages of their sin was death—visited upon the succeeding generation. What began in pleasure ended in tantamount anguish and pain. That was the first consequence of David's sin.

Some time later Amnon raped his own sister Tamar. Both were David's own children. The awful blotch of enmity, abuse, incest, and betrayal had now been visited in full measure against the house of David. Again, what was supposed to be the wellspring of joy had become the headwaters of pain. That was the second consequence of David's sin.

Absolom, another of David's sons, upon hearing what Amnon did to Tamar, killed his brother. David's sin had cost him the life of Bathsheba's firstborn. It had cost him the harmony and integrity of his family. Now, it had cost him the life of another son. That was the third consequence of his sin.

And if that were not enough, shortly thereafter, Absolom revolted against his father, David. He tried to take over the throne. During the rebellion, Absolom was killed by those loyal to the king. David wept over the body of his son, saying, "Absolom, oh Absolom, would to God I could have died in your stead, oh Absolom, my son." He had now lost three of his sons and witnessed the utter decimation of his family. That was the fourth consequence of his sin.

Sadly, the sins of parents are often passed on to children. Our foolishness and rebellion doesn't simply affect us. It affects all those around us—and it most fully affects those closest to us.

Before any of us chooses to pursue the path of sin, we should carefully review its consequences. In those moments when we might be anticipating illicit pleasures of the flesh, thinking of ways to satisfy our desires outside the parameters of God's will, or harboring selfish passions, if we would only review the consequences, we would realize the curse of sin—and hopefully, we would recoil in horror. Sin is never worth the consequences it brings.

REGARD THE CONVICTION OF SIN

The thing David had done was evil in the sight of God, but until the prophet Nathan pointed it out, David didn't have ears to hear. He didn't have eyes to see. He was unable to comprehend the truth. David was so full of sin that he didn't realize Nathan was bringing an indictment against him. He was so fixed on the appeasement of his own concerns that he was utterly devoid of spiritual discernment.

Yet by the time Nathan concluded his covenant lawsuit, David's eyes were opened; conviction had gripped his heart and mind. At that point, David actually accepted the blame. He knew that it wasn't the circumstances; it wasn't the situation; it wasn't the peer pressure; it wasn't the devil. He took responsibility: he realized he was to blame, and the convicting power of the holy God fell on him.

God knows us all. He knew us before the foundation of the world. He knows where we were Friday night and what we did. God knows everything about us—and yet He still loves us. Indeed, that is amazing grace.

David confessed his sin in genuine repentance. "I have sinned against the Lord," he wailed. None of us are to the place of confession until we recognize that we are to blame for our sin, until we take responsibility for our sin and stop blaming others.

David confessed his sin, and that was the beginning of his restoration. He accepted the cleansing that comes only in accord with God's good providence. Though he couldn't erase the damage he had caused and undo the havoc he had wrecked, he could have a fresh new start—as hard as that might be given the stern consequences of his sin.

It is no wonder so many of us are without purpose and joy and power and victorious Christian living. The terrible thing about sin is that when we sin, we are not merely sinning against our children, our wife, our husband, our rival, or our enemy. When we sin we are, first and foremost, sinning against the Lord.

David realized this—and thus, he began the passage from death to life once again. He heard the Word of God as it spoke clearly and decisively to his situation. He immediately realized the fullness of his own sin. He immediately recognized the consequences of the wickedness he had wrought. His heart was pierced, at last.

He was, after all, David. Though he had fallen from the pinnacle of his earlier success, he was a man who knew how to pursue the heart of God. He was a man who was familiar with the courtyard of grace and the threshold of hope. He knew well the parameters of everlasting joy. He had once been a frequent guest of the Great Shepherd's green pastures and still waters. So, when David heard the Word of truth, he was stricken.

Then came conviction.

And then came repentance—and with repentance came the gracious environs of hope.

Moral Soundings

- Have you fully recognized the cause of sin in your life?
- Have you ever come to grips with the awfulness of the curse of sin?
- Have you ever calculated the full dimensions of sin's consequences?
- How do you regard the conviction of sin?
- How long has it been since you have done what David did, and confessed your sin?

–10–

Transgressions, Iniquities, and Sins

*Have mercy on me, O God,
according to your unfailing love.*
Psalm 51:1

In the aftermath of an earthquake—or any other natural disaster, for that matter—people inevitably second-guess themselves. "Why wasn't I home when it happened? If I had only been there, maybe we wouldn't have lost everything. Why didn't we take out that extra insurance when we had the chance last year? Why didn't we put our valuables in the safety deposit box at the bank? Why did I let the kids stay home on this day, of all days?" Why, oh why?

Hindsight is 20/20. We beat ourselves up equally over minor omissions and major commissions. We torture ourselves with regret, with remorse, and with recalcitrance. We agonize over what could have been or what should have been.

If that is the case with a geological earthquake, how much more is it the case with a moral earthquake. Guilt, blame, and sorrow necessarily hang over the aftermath of our moral failures, moral ruptures, and moral collapses. They are the natural companions of sin-provoked tragedy.

No doubt, David dealt with all that and more in the aftermath of his moral earthquake. But instead of wallowing in his grief, he sought relief in the mercy of God.

The record of his recovery process is a marvel to behold. For every one of us who must journey through this poor fallen world, it is a tremendous encouragement. It enables us to get past the second-guessing, the brow-beating, and the soul-searching. It enables us to see past the ruin and rubble we have made of our circumstances and get on with life.

In fact, Psalm 51—the stunningly transparent passage that offers a glimpse of David's repentance and recovery—was written not merely for private prayer but as a public song. In his brilliant commentary on the Book of Psalms, *The Treasury of David*, Charles Spurgeon asserts that this psalm is equally suitable for individual penitence and for an entire assembly. It gives voice to our deepest longings for forgiveness and rest—whether we are alone in our closet or arrayed around the throne with the whole congregation of the Lord.

THE UNIVERSAL CRY

The psalm was written after Nathan the prophet came to David and confronted him with his sin (see 2 Sam. 11–12). Nathan's message had reawakened David's hardened heart and made him see the greatness of his guilt. As a result, the once-prolific troubadour of the Lord returned to his long-forgotten harp and poured out this song—accompanied with various sighs and tears.

David speaks specifically about three slights he had committed against the integrity of the Lord: transgressions, iniquities, and sins. He clearly differentiates between these three violations. Then he asks God to deal with those breaches in ways appropriate to each: to blot out his transgressions, to wash his iniquities, and to cleanse his sins.

In this regard, Psalm 51 is a substantive paradigm for the prayer of forgiveness. Not surprisingly, it has always been recognized as such. Only heaven has recorded how many thousands and thousands of believers through the centuries have come to this psalm and prayed it as their own—for it expresses the universal cry for mercy in the midst of the calamity of a moral earthquake.

It contains a message that is both forthright and obvious: any of us—from the little child, who tells what we call a "fib," to the vilest of sinners—can appeal to God for forgiveness and the restoration of a joyous life of service if we simply come to Him with a contriteness of mind, with a brokenness of spirit, and with a true heart intent on unrestrained repentance.

CONFESSION

David begins his remarkable journey of recovery and repentance with a heartfelt confession of sin. Thus, he appeals to the mercy of God.

Isaiah the prophet asked: "The Lord's hand is not so short that it cannot save; neither is His ear so dull that it cannot hear. But your iniquities have made a separation between you and your God . . . so that he does not hear" (59:1–2, NASB).

So often we rush into prayer with things in our heart and life that we haven't asked God to blot out or cleanse away, and then wonder why we can't get the ear of God, why we can't live a victorious Christian life.

David begins his prayer with a recognition that his rebellion has separated him from the Lord. He appeals for an audience in the throne room of heaven by entering with confession on his lips: "Have mercy on me, O God, according to your unfailing love; according to your great compassion blot out my transgressions" (Ps. 51:1, NIV).

He didn't appeal to God on the basis of judgment, and he certainly didn't come on the basis of merit. He didn't come to God and say, "Hey, look at all the wonderful things I've done in the past for the sake of your name and your kingdom. Let's just put all of my good deeds over here on a scale. Oh sure, I've blown it in a few areas, but look how many more good deeds I've done."

It is a dangerous thing to move off the ground of grace. God does not grade on the curve. He doesn't populate His kingdom by percentages and comparisons. The fact is, none of us deserve anything from Him. We are able to approach Him solely and completely because of His tender mercies. Thus, David appeals to the God of "unfailing love" and of "great compassion." There is no pretense or implication of just desserts.

David initiates his soulful prayer with a full recognition of the fact that he does not deserve forgiveness—not in the least. Thus, he can only appeal for mercy. There is no other ground for negotiation. Mercy is not getting what we deserve. Mercy is not getting what is fair. Mercy is altogether the gracious gift of our long-suffering sovereign God.

So, David prays, "Blot out my transgressions." The Hebrew word for "transgressions" appears nearly a hundred times in the Old Testament. It literally means "to rebel, to revolt, or to cross over the line." It describes a gross violation of the law, not merely a slight omission or a piddling mistake. It describes a spirit of defiant disobedience to authority. Transgressions are flagrant, deliberate, premeditated breaches of a clear standard. It is not irresponsibility; it is rebellion.

David admits that his sin was indeed a transgression. There were no ifs, ands, or buts about it. David deliberately set his face against the clearly revealed will of God. He sinned. He rebelled. He knew precisely what he was doing the whole time he was doing it, and he admits as much. He says, "I've stepped over the line. I've transgressed. I've revolted. I've rebelled. I've been disobedient."

On that basis—without even a hint of hedging, justifying, or conditioning—David asks God to blot out those awful transgressions. The Hebrew word translated "blot out" literally means "to wipe away or to utterly erase." It was used by Moses when he appealed to God for the nation of Israel. As he stood on Mount Sinai in the stead of his people, he said: "But now, please forgive their sin—but if not, then blot me out of the book you have written" (Exod. 32:32, NIV).

Later, it was used to describe a man who wipes a dish on one side and then turns it over and wipes it again (2 Kings 21:13).

All of us know firsthand the agonizing experience of stepping over the line. Each of us has deliberately, self-consciously, purposefully rebelled against God. We have no excuses. We cannot rectify our violation of the integrity of God. We cannot justify our actions in any way. We are left entirely to the mercy of God, and what does He do in the face of such blatant sin? Like an accountant erasing a mistake, God blots out our transgressions. He erases them from the ledger altogether. He wipes them clean so that they look brand-new and spotless. It is almost as if the besmirching of our character had never occurred.

INIQUITIES

Having dealt with his transgressions, David now focuses on a different aspect of his sin. Not only had he stepped over the line and transgressed, he had also defiled and soiled himself with iniquity. So he prayed: "Wash away all my iniquity and cleanse me from my sin" (Ps. 51:2, NIV).

In the original Hebrew text, the word translated "iniquity" literally means "to bend, to twist, to distort." Elihu utilized the same word when the sinner confessed that he had "perverted what was right" (Job 33:27). It was also expressively employed by Jeremiah the prophet to describe the opposite of the straight and narrow way of a righteous life—it was, instead, the crooked pathway of wickedness (Lam. 3:9).

David confesses that he has not only transgressed the perfect standards of God, he has twisted and distorted his calling and destiny in life. He has gone by the wayside. He has perverted and polluted his providential purpose in life. Though all the damage cannot be undone, and all his squandered benefits cannot be fully reinstated, he knows that something must be done. His twisted perversion and the vile pollution of his iniquities must be dealt with.

So, David asks God to wash him thoroughly. The Hebrew verb we translate "wash" is almost always used to describe the "cleaning of clothes" or the "removal of stains." David asks God to wash him like a dirty shirt. Notice, he desires not only his clothing to be washed, but he pleads: "Wash me." While the casual sinner is content with a light dusting off, the truly-awakened conscience desires a complete and efficient washing. One sin pollutes our entire nature. One breach covers us with filth and entirely distorts our purpose in life. It twists our countenance beyond recognition.

Thus, we must deal seriously with sin, just as David does. Iniquities must be washed.

SINS

David moves from transgressions to iniquities to sins. Not only had he stepped over the line and transgressed, not only had he defiled and twisted his calling and purpose with iniquity, but he had also fallen short of the mark and sullied his soul—he had sinned. So he prays: "Wash away all my iniquity and cleanse me from my sin" (Ps. 51:2, NIV).

The word David chooses to express the idea of "sin" is used almost three hundred times in the Old Testament. The first mention of it was in the story of Cain and Abel. There we read, "If you do not do well, sin lies at the door" (Gen. 4:7). This Hebrew word is much like it's New Testament equivalent. It literally means "missing the mark." It illustrates a failed attempt to shoot at a bull's-eye—the arrow flies away from the intended target and completely misses the mark. David admits, "That is what I have done."

Notice that his "transgressions" were plural—all the times that he had stepped over the line. But they are replaced by the singular "sin" here. All his many transgressions had each sprung from a common root—sin. Later in this magnificent prayer, he expresses this profound truth: "I was brought forth in iniquity, and in sin my mother conceived me" (Ps. 51: 5). All our transgressions spring from a common root—that sin nature in which we were born.

David asks God to cleanse him. The word he uses for "cleanse" literally means "to scour, to purify, or to depurate." It describes the process of "purging" or of "absolution." It also appears in the story of Naaman, who had leprosy. He was told to dip seven times in the Jordan and he would be clean (see 2 Kings 5). If he did as he was told, he would be purified, and the disease would be purged from his body.

Before David asks God for anything else, before he petitions the throne for any other prerogatives, before he makes supplication for any other matter—before he petitions God to create in him a clean heart or renew within him a steadfast spirit or return to him the joy of his salvation—he appeals for mercy in the face of his defiled estate. He asks to be cleansed of his filthiness.

ACCEPTING RESPONSIBILITY

David takes the full blame for his transgressions, iniquities, and sins. Notice the personal pronouns he uses: my transgressions, my iniquities, my sins. There is no one to blame for his foolish acts of rebellion—and he doesn't even try. There is no psychoanalysis, no probing into his past, no discussion of all the pressure he'd been under, no consideration of how lonely it is at the top. David refuses to play the blame game. He knows it wasn't the devil, his circumstances, or anything else that caused his moral earthquake. He knows the responsibility is all his—and he accepts it.

Apparently, this reality was inescapable for David; it hounded him. Though it had been nearly a year since the calamity of his sin, he admits, "My sin is always before me" (Ps. 51:3). It continued to haunt him. He says: "Against You, You only, have I sinned, and done this evil in your sight—so that You may be just when You speak, and blameless when You judge" (Ps. 51:4). David acknowledges that he had crossed the line God had drawn for his life. He acknowledges his transgressions.

It is tragic how so few people really get to this place. Some of us are pretty good at acknowledging sin—as long as it is not our sin that we are acknowledging. It is easy to confess the sins of others, and we're pretty good at acknowledging the sins of the church. We're certainly opinionated about acknowledging the sins of the nation, but most of us find it difficult to say, "I'm the one. I did it. I'm guilty." David wasn't caught up in the transgressions of anyone else. His own transgressions had been hounding him. He says, "My sin is always before me." Apparently, everywhere he turned he saw the ghost of his rebellious past. He saw it in the eyes of the people around him. He lived with it for twelve months. He thought about it at night, lying in the darkness before he went to sleep.

That is one of the most debilitating things about unconfessed sin. It hounds us. Until he got to the place of confession and repentance that we find in this psalm, David lived nearly a year with his sin hounding him. Every day was spent looking over his shoulder, wondering if he was going to be found out, telling one lie to cover another, and yet another to cover that one. His sin had begun to dominate his every waking moment.

Not only did he discover that sin hounds the sinner, it also haunts him. "Against You, God, and You only have I sinned," he confesses. A casual observer might have objected, "I thought his sin was against Uriah. He stole his wife. He stole from Uriah. And, as if that were not bad enough, he took Uriah's life." Another might disagree, saying, "I thought his sin was against Bathsheba. He initiated this affair. He brought her up into his palace and wooed her, persuaded her, and seduced her." Still another might say, "I thought his sin was against the innocent baby that never had a chance to live because of his father's sin."

But according to David, the most heinous aspect of his sin was that it was an assault on God's integrity. The thought that haunted him the most was that his sin was an affront to God. Indeed, though he certainly took advantage of those around him, his primary offense was against God—because all sin is first and foremost a violation of His standards.

This really is the horrible thing about crossing the line—transgressing. This is the great tragedy of twisting the truth, of going the crooked way, and of missing the mark. This is the horrible, haunting thing about it: at the root of it all, our sin is an offense against God.

Do we realize that when we talk back to our parents it is a sin against God? Do we realize when we cut corners on our IRS return, that we've not only cheated the government of the United States, but we have sinned against God?

Like the prodigal son, David confesses, "I have sinned against heaven, and before thee, and am no more worthy to be called thy son" (Luke 15:18–19). Nevertheless, he repented; and like the prodigal son, he was able to return home—not as a hired servant or a second-class citizen. He was able to return home as an honored son.

That is the way God takes us back. We don't have to live being hounded and haunted by our transgressions. We can go home— and there find forgiveness and rest.

David was genuinely sorrowful. He was grieved over his transgressions, iniquities, and sins. Not once does he attempt to justify his sin or give excuses. David was not just sorry he got caught; he was sorry for what he had done against God.

"Surely I have been a sinner from birth," he prayed, "sinful from the time my mother conceived me" (Psalm 51:5, NIV).

David acknowledged that he was born with a sinful nature. We must ask ourselves this question: Are we a sinner because we have sinned or do we sin because we are sinners? A lot of people think we are all born good. Then, because of our environment or other factors, our pure primordial goodness is somehow contaminated. They suppose that it is some external pressure that manages to drag us down. They believe that the pressure of the world provokes us to act badly from time to time, but that such behavior is actually out of the norm for us.

David doesn't pull any of these punches. He places the blame squarely where it belongs—with himself. He says, "I sin because I'm a sinner. I was born that way." With the apostle Paul, he says: "Therefore, just as sin entered the world through one man, and death through sin, and in this way death came to all men, because all sinned" (Rom. 5:12, NIV). And with the prophet Isaiah he asserts: "We all, like sheep, have gone astray, each of us has turned to his own way; and the LORD has laid on him the iniquity of us all" (Isa. 53:6, NIV).

The Bible says we are born with this inherent sinful nature. But doesn't man have a free will? Yes, we have a free will, we are free to do what we want to do. And you know what we want to do? We want to sin. We're born with that sinful nature. This is what the great reformer Martin Luther called the "bondage of the will." A little baby that doesn't get satisfied with a bottle at the right time doubles up her fist and throws a tantrum.

David faces this fact clearly. He sees the cataclysm of his life in light of this great truth. He confesses. Thus, he finds light and life.

Moral Soundings

- Do you see the difference between transgressions, iniquities, and sins?
- Have you appropriated God's provision for blotting, washing, and cleansing?
- Have you accepted full responsibility for your past actions.
- Have you come to terms with your sinful nature and your need for God's mercy?
- Have you ever prayed through this prayer of David's in the aftermath of a moral earthquake?

–11–

WASHED CLEAN

Cleanse me with hyssop,
and I will be clean.
Psalm 51:7, NIV

≥≈

In the aftermath of the 1989 Bay Area earthquake, property owners got a quick lesson in insurance claims. To their horror they discovered that not only were they forced to dig out from under a mountain of rubble, they had to dig out from under a mountain of red tape as well.

Calls were not returned. Adjusters failed to show up, and promises were not kept. As a result, the patience of many claimants wore thin. It was just another example of the squeaky wheel getting the grease. In order to get a quick response from their agents and adjusters, they discovered that they had to persistently, constantly, and insistently ask.

In Psalm 51, we see this same sort of supplication in the life of David. He doesn't give up. Despite the grievousness of his sin, he remains persistent, constant, and insistent.

At the heart of his prayer of confession was a whole series of requests. David asks God to purge him—to cleanse him—from all of that sin. He asks God to wash him. He asks God to let him hear and see again. He asks God to set aright his body, soul, and spirit.

Ask: a simple little one-syllable word. It is a basic concept— such a simple thing to do. To ask someone for something is no great thing—at least, at first glance it doesn't appear to be. Isn't it strange, then, that we attempt to live out our lives only asking others for things when we absolutely have to? Some of us are just too proud to ask for anything—even too proud to ask God for anything.

Yet, the Lord Jesus taught us, His children, to ask: "Ask and it will be given to you; seek and you will find; knock and the door will be opened to you" (Matt. 7:7, NIV).

The apostle James said, "You do have because you do not ask." While, he added, "You ask and do not receive, because you ask amiss, that you may spend it on your pleasures" (James 4:2–3).

David avoids both extremes. He asks God for His covenant blessings. He asks aright, pleading the cause of righteousness: "Purge me with hyssop, and I shall be clean; wash me, and I shall be whiter than snow. Make me hear joy and gladness, that the bones You have broken may rejoice. Hide Your face from my sins, and blot out all my iniquities. Create in me a clean heart, O God, and renew a steadfast spirit within me. Do not cast me away from Your presence, and do not take Your Holy Spirit from me. Restore to me the joy of Your salvation, and uphold me by Your generous Spirit" (Ps. 51:7–12).

Notice the verbs David employs in his great supplication: *cleanse* me, *wash* me, *make* me, *create* me, *renew* me, and *restore* me. Together, these active requests form the heart and soul of David's repentance.

CLEANSE ME

King David felt soiled, dirty, and stained. He knew that neither ritual, religion, resolve, nor reform could cleanse his sin-stained soul. It was deeply stained, so he asks God to cleanse him with hyssop. The word he uses literally means "to purge or to expunge." It is a word used to describe not merely a ritual, cursory dusting off; it does not describe something that is simply rinsed off, like a dish under running water. Instead, it describes a thorough scrubbing, scouring, and purifying. It comes closest to our word *sterilizing*.

Thus, he prays, "Cleanse me with hyssop." If we go to Jerusalem today, we can walk into the Old City through the Dung Gates, near where the Western Wall is, and find hyssop. It is an herb that grows naturally there; in fact, you may discover it growing out of the walls of the city. But in the Old Testament, hyssop was not simply a common herb. It was an integral part of Israel's ritual worship. In the ceremonial section of the Mosaic Law, hyssop was used in the ceremonial cleaning of lepers. It was also used by the Levitical priests during sacrifices in the temple to take blood and sprinkle it on the altar.

David asks God to cleanse him thoroughly—to purge him with hyssop, just as the priest did during the worship services held in the temple. He could stand his uncleanness and filth no more.

The prophet Isaiah records God's own plea to us all: "'Come now, and let us reason together,' says the Lord. 'Though your sins are like scarlet, they shall be as white as snow; though they are red like crimson, they shall be as wool'" (Isa. 1:18).

Some of us want to be whitewashed instead of washed white. When we are simply whitewashed, we cover up the marred surface of our lives; we merely hide the blotches and scars. But when we are washed white, all of those stains are actually removed— they cease to exist altogether. David doesn't want a bit of a cover up. He is not interested in simply skirting the consequences of his sin. He wants to deal with it—substantively. He wants to eradicate the last vestiges of his sin. He wants to be clean—from the inside out. He wants to be thoroughly washed.

The great Victorian preacher Charles Spurgeon asked, "Is there a verse in all of Scripture more full of faith than this?" Indeed, this is a passage that radiates a full and vivacious faith, a faith rooted in the grace and mercy of God Almighty. "Purge me with hyssop and I shall be clean, wash me and I shall be whiter than snow." If we all really believed that, what a difference it would make.

David is a man whose sin has greatly stained his soul. Now he asks to be purged and washed. Some of us are too proud to do that. That is precisely why so many of us remain encumbered by the sins of our past. It is the very reason why some of us are not free—we have not asked.

JOY AND GLADNESS

David's supplications do not end with his request to be washed clean, but he goes on to ask for a measure of restoration: "Let me hear joy and gladness; let the bones you have crushed rejoice" (Ps. 51:8, NIV). During the tenure of his great apostasy and rebellion, David had become deaf to the voice of God. But now, in his repentance, he requests ears to hear.

Can you imagine? The man after God's own heart had allowed the embers of his faith to go cold—to the point of extinction. That is what sin does. At one time, David could take his harp and make the palace resonate with sounds of joy and gladness, but sin had so hardened his sensibilities that he had become spiritually tone deaf. He had become utterly deaf to the sounds of joy. That is what sin will always do to us. It will take away our song. It will take away our joy. It will steal the music of love, joy, peace, patience, kindness, and goodness from our lives. It will crowd our senses with the cacophonous din of this poor fallen world, while the sweet strains of heaven will be pitched beyond our hearing.

David knew full well what it was to hear the songs of deliverance, but his rebellion had so scarred him that he could no longer detect their strains. It must have been rather like the fellow who left the ministry and was asked sometime later what it was he missed the most. He said, "The thing I miss the most is hearing the trumpets in the morning—calling me to service." David missed the morning clarions. He missed the trumpets of joy and gladness, and so he asks God to enable him to somehow hear them once again.

OUT OF SIGHT

Again, David does not stop there. He continues to ask. He continues to make supplication. He continues to make his requests known. He prays: "Hide your face from my sins, and blot out all my iniquities."

It is a terrible thing to be found out in sin. We see this all the time on the human level. A man is captured, suspected by the police of committing a particular crime. As he is being taken into the police station, he covers his face in an attempt to avoid the leering cameras broadcasting into thousands of homes all across town. He walks into the police station with a newspaper shielding his face. He doesn't want the cameras to capture his image, so he hides it. He is ashamed.

David was ashamed. He had been exposed. He was naked and vulnerable. The gaze of the immutable, incomprehensible, immortal God was trained directly upon him in his miserable estate. It was almost more than he could possibly bear, and he felt the burning anguish of shame.

One of the greatest tragedies of American Christianity is that we've lost our shame. We have become both callous and brazen. We even attach a bit of mystique to bold sinning, but shame was a character trait that was by no means lost on David.

So he cries out for mercy. "Cleanse me," he cries. "Wash me. Blot out. Hide your face from the blight of my rebellion." David knew only too well that if God does not graciously blot out our sins, He will necessarily blot out something else—our names from the book of life. He must do one or the other. Justice demands that sin be dealt with. It simply cannot be passed over. God cannot simply avert His gaze. God cannot simply look past our failures and foibles. All must be dealt with; otherwise, His all-holy character is compromised.

A CLEAN HEART

Still, David does not stop there. He asks for yet more. He prays: "Create in me a clean heart, O God, and renew a steadfast spirit within me" (Ps. 51:8).

In the Hebrew language there are several different words that can be translated "create." In this case, it is the word used in the very first verse in the Bible: "In the beginning, God created the heavens and the earth." It literally means "to make or fashion out of nothing." In the context of Genesis, it simply describes the way God called forth existence out of absolute nothingness. The entire cosmos was fabricated by the very breath of His mouth. He simply spoke and it was so.

The word is thus demonstrative of the fact that the creative activity of God can bring something out of nothing. And that is exactly what David asks Him to do. The word indicates something that a human being could never do for himself. David could never create in himself a clean heart—anymore than any of us can, as much as we might try.

Notice, David is not asking for some kind of restoration. He doesn't say, "Give me back what I've lost. Restore what the erosion of sin has stripped from my heart." He wants regeneration. He is asking for an entirely new heart. He is saying, "Create what is not there. Create what never was there. Don't just bring me back up to speed. I need an altogether new heart."

Man always tries to start his reform efforts on the outside and work inward. God always begins on the inside and works outward. Jesus says, "For out of the heart come evil thoughts, murder, adultery, sexual immorality, theft, false testimony, slander" (Matt. 15:19, NIV). David knew that he needed to guard against future moral earthquakes, so he wants more than simply a return to the status quo. He asks for a steadfast spirit.

The most important thing about a man is his spirit. We can have all kinds of degrees, pedigrees, and experiences, but if we don't have a right spirit, God can't use us. King David knew this.

IN HIS PRESENCE

Even now though, David was not through making his petitions and requests. He asks for yet more: "Do not cast me away from Your presence, and do not take Your Holy Spirit from me. Restore to me the joy of Your salvation, and uphold me by Your generous Spirit" (Ps. 51:11–12).

Here, the sinner king confronts his greatest fear and expresses his highest aspiration. Thus, the language becomes rather emphatic—notice the *dos* and the *don'ts*. He says, "Don't cast me away from your presence," and "Don't take your Holy Spirit from me." Simultaneously he says, "Do restore to me the joy of your salvation," and "do uphold me by your generous Spirit."

This emphatic list of dos and don'ts really exposes David's heart in a remarkable way. They reveal his real agenda, his highest priorities, and his greatest anxieties. They paint a vivid portrait of his heart in transition—from the devastation of a moral earthquake to the restoration of a character of humble discipleship.

Clearly, David's great fear was that God might abandon him, that God might cast him away from His presence. It was that he might be left entirely to himself. He knew that he was responsible for cutting off fellowship with God in the first place. He knew that God was faithful—it was David who had been faithless. He simply feared that he may have gone too far over the line. He feared that he might have crossed a kind of ultimate and final threshold and that he would not be able to recover. He had given up on God—he was now afraid that perhaps God would give up on him in return. You can almost hear him lament, "Don't cast me away as you did Cain." After all, one of the saddest verses in all the Bible says, "Cain went out from the presence of the Lord" (Gen. 4:16).

David did not want the same to be said of him. In addition, he was afraid that he was no longer to have the presence or power of the Holy Spirit, so he prays, "Do not take your Holy Spirit from me."

What would it be like to have no Comforter? Where would we be with no Teacher? How would we function if we were forced to come to the Bible and read it without the Holy Spirit to open our eyes to behold its wondrous truths? How could we comprehend it without the Holy Spirit to open our hearts?

To know the presence of the Holy Spirit and then to be cast away from that presence would be more than any of us could possibly bear. To know what it is to have a Comforter, a Teacher, and then to suddenly to be bereft of that privilege would be calamitous. To have no guide when we come to a crisis in life is a horror to deep and too profound to fully fathom. No wonder David shuddered at the thought.

David's heartfelt cry echoes across the centuries—these aren't just words. David expresses the greatest fear of his life. To have the Holy Spirit is to have faith, hope, and love. But bar the Spirit and we're left without faith—thus we can only be skeptical. Bar the Spirit and we're left without hope—thus we can only be disillusioned. Bar the Spirit and we're left without love—thus we can only be cynical. Sadly, we have all known people like that: skeptical, disillusioned, and cynical with no power in the present because they have no perspective of the past or vision for the future.

Think of it: to have known the sweet Holy Spirit, and then to lose Him! Such a fate would be worse than a musician losing his music, or a writer losing his pen, or a singer losing his song—all never able to do what they do or be what they are ever again. It is worse even than a man losing his country—never able to return home again.

Jewish culture is resplendent with a rich tradition of stories, legends, and fables. One story about the A.D. 70 destruction of Jerusalem—that occurred nearly forty years after Christ's crucifixion when Titus and his Roman legions sacked the city—is especially poignant. According to tradition, just before the final assault, loud, mysterious voices were heard echoing in the Temple. "Let us depart," they announced; afterward, a great sound of unearthly wings, sweeping across a darkened sky, was heard. According to rabbis through the ages, this was Jehovah and His angels abandoning a disobedient city to its own fate—withdrawing from a Temple that failed to give Him honor.

Legend? No doubt. But what about human temples? What about us? Have we ever made the dwelling place of the Most High so cluttered with the rubbish and perversities of this world that it is no longer fit for His presence?

That is the very thing David feared most. David knew what it was to commune with the Holy Spirit in times past. In the economy of the Old Testament, the Holy Spirit sometimes was taken from men when they were disobedient or unfaithful. For example, the Spirit of God departed from Samson and from Saul.

In our dispensation, however, the Holy Spirit comes to in-dwell the believer at the moment of conversion, to empower us for service, to give us gifts of ministry, to comfort us and to teach us, to guide us, fill us, and to live His life out through us; He has promised that He will never leave us.

A Christian may be cast away from service. In 1 Corinthians 9:27, that was Paul's fear—that he might become a castaway. But the Holy Spirit will not leave us. A child of God in this dispensation never has to fear that happening.

Of course, David does not conclude on a negative note—but a positive one. He doesn't end his great plea with his fears—but with his hopes. He doesn't wind up with don'ts—but with dos. So David says, "Do restore to me the joy of your salvation," and "do uphold me by your generous Spirit." The fact is, if God would grant His Spirit, then this final request would most assuredly be fulfilled.

Indeed, it was; and indeed it is.

Moral Soundings

- Are you bold enough to go before the throne of God and ask—simply ask?
- Are your requests generally about things? Or are they like David's, about your own character?
- Have the strains of joy and faith become little more than dim memories to you?
- Can you identify with David's greatest fears—or his greatest aspirations?
- The Holy Spirit has not abandoned you; have you abandoned Him?

-12-

RESTORING JOY

Restore to me the joy of Your salvation.
Psalm 51:12

ॐ

The red tape of bureaucracy drove the official in charge of rebuilding the earthquake-shattered city of Kobe to commit suicide. Government spokesmen reported that Deputy Mayor Takumi Ogawa—who was in charge of reconstructing the city after the worst natural disaster in Japan this century—set himself on fire after a frustrating year of rebuilding. Local officials had long criticized the central government for being too slow to respond to the disaster with money to help the city recover. Apparently, Ogawa simply was unable to see how things would—or even could—get better.

Anyone who has ever suffered a moral earthquake might be tempted to sympathize. There is a kind of smothering grief that attends such a disaster. Often the aftermath can be as bad or worse than the original event.

It is not surprising then to see David crying out to God—in the aftermath of his moral earthquake—to bring him relief from his unrelenting agony: "Restore to me the joy of Your salvation, and uphold me by Your generous Spirit" (Ps. 51:12)

It is a prayer of the heart—one that any of us who have suffered a moral earthquake can readily identify with. The fact is, while we

126

can't lose our salvation, we can certainly lose our joy. And in the face of a moral earthquake, we inevitably do. David did; therefore, he cries out to God for relief. In so doing, he provides a model for us to do likewise. We need not end our lives in despair. We can recover the great joy of our salvation and find our support in the gracious and generous trusses of the Spirit.

HIS JOY

David does not ask for God to restore his salvation. Believers— those of us who live this side of Calvary, who put our faith in Jesus Christ—are eternally secure in Him. But even though we can't lose our salvation, we certainly can lose the joy of our salvation.

David prays this great prayer of repentance and confession because he has gotten his life out of order. He has put himself first in his life. As a result, he has done something very selfish. So now he prays for the joy of God's salvation to be restored to him.

King David takes his depression to God. He knows it was caused by sin, and he admits as much. Some people never have their joy restored, even though they spend a fortune, going to counselors and reading every book they can read. We live in a world where it seems that our troubles are always someone else's fault; someone else is always to blame. Very few people want to take personal responsibility for their foolish actions, for their deliberate trans-gressions, for their blatant sins, or for their brazen iniquities. But David does not even hesitate. He knows the truth of his own heart. He knows that his troubles are all his fault. He understands the fact that his moral earthquake was set off by secret moral faults that lay hidden beneath the surface of his seemingly very successful life. Thus, he confesses to the Lord, "Against You, You only, have I sinned" (Ps. 51:4).

But now David asks God to let him know the peace and rest that he once enjoyed. Joy is one of the real characteristics of a Christian. However, when we indulge in sin, we jeopardize that joy. Sin and rebellion inevitably cost us the inheritance of joy that is ours in Christ. A Christian may lose the joy of his salvation without losing his salvation.

The joy had left King David because he had sinned, and because he had tried for a period of several months to cover over that sin.

The same thing happens to each of us when we fall into the clutches of temptation and sin. Those of us who know Christ as our personal Savior, who nevertheless live in sin, will most assuredly lose the joy of salvation. To try to cover up our transgressions, iniquities, and sins—to minimize them, to excuse them, or to justify them—will undoubtedly lead to heart-sickness, sorrow, and sadness. Perpetuating sin only leads to a loss of the joy of God's gracious and glorious work of salvation.

So, how can the process be reversed? How does the restoration of joy take place? In a word—*grace*. This amazing notion is illustrated all throughout David's great prayer of repentance and confession, as we have already seen. The new heart David needed to receive joy could only come from God. The cleansing, the purging, the blotting, and the hearkening that needed to take place in his life could only be accomplished by the sovereign work of God's gracious hand.

Notice precisely what it is that David asks for. He says, "Restore to me the joy of Your salvation." It's God's joy, it's God's salvation that is at issue here, not David's joy, not David's salvation. All the attention is on God, not on the poor helpless sinner. The focus is shifted to the One who can make a difference, the One who can make all the difference. No one but God can give us the kind of joy David seeks.

SUSTENANCE

In addition to the restoration of God's great joy, David asks for the sustenance of His hand and His Spirit. He prays: "And uphold me by Your generous Spirit" (Ps. 51:12).

King David realizes that his only hope is for God to keep him, for God to uphold him. He cannot do it on his own. He wants to never again fall into that situation, so he tells God he will depend solely and completely on Him. He asks God to uphold him by His generous spirit.

The word translated "uphold" here is quite interesting. It is an architectural term for a pillar or column. For instance, it is used to describe the way Samson took hold of the two pillars upon which the great Philistine palace was borne up (see Judg. 16:29).

In a sense, David is asking God, "Uphold me, just like a father would uphold his child when teaching him to walk—not just letting him grab his fingers so he has to hold on, but reaching down and grabbing him by the wrist so that when he stumbles, he holds him up along the way."

God is so generous in his gifts to us, so forgiving, so full of grace, and so full of tender mercy. In this dispensation of His grace, we never have to pray, "Don't cast me away from your presence, and do not take your Holy Spirit from me." Why? Because we have been afforded the great privilege of praying, "Restore to me the joy of your salvation, and uphold me by your generous Spirit."

NOTORIOUS REPENTANCE

When is a man usable? When his repentance is as notorious as his sin. The prophet Nathan boldly confronted David in the spirit of grace and truth. Almost immediately, David's heart was broken. His eyes were opened. And, after a year of sinful rebellion, he suddenly turned in humble repentance. He fell on his knees and began to pray a prayer that was subsequently recorded for all posterity—the prayer of repentance and confession we find in Psalm 51.

His repentance was notorious, as notorious as his sin. As a result, God was able to use him again.

Some people try to make deals with God. They say, "God create in me a clean heart and don't cast me away. Restore the joy of your salvation to me. If you do all that, then I'll teach transgressors; I'll sing your praises and my tongue shall sing aloud of your business; my mouth shall show forth your praise." David was not making a deal with God here. Instead, he simply said, "Not until I'm washed clean, not until I have a new heart and a steadfast spirit within me, not until I've been restored unto the joy of your salvation, not until then will I be able to do what I want to do: teach transgressors your ways, letting my mouth and my lips sing forth of your praises and your righteousness." There is no deal here. There is simply an acknowledgment of what grace produces in a life fully yielded to God's good providence.

THE FRUIT OF FORGIVENESS

What happens when one finds the forgiveness of God? David's great prayer portrays not only our dire need of grace and mercy, but the happy result of grace and mercy in our lives.

In the first half of the prayer, David pours out his heart: "Wash me," he says. "Blot out my transgressions. Cleanse me. I acknowledge my wickedness. My sin is ever before me. I was brought forth in iniquity. Wash me and I'll be whiter than snow. Hide your face from my sins. Create in me a clean heart." Over and over and over David issues forth a constant cry for God to forgive him of his sin. He uncovers himself so that God can cover him. But the second half of the prayer portrays a threefold commitment to a new life of dedication, a fresh hunger to undertake three essential discipleship tasks: education, exaltation, and exhortation.

When we've come clean before God and have received cleansing, one of the results is that we begin to live a life dedicated to education. David says, "Then I will teach transgressors Your ways" (Ps. 51:13).

THE SCHOOL OF HARD KNOCKS

There is nothing more dynamic about someone who has just tasted the forgiveness of God than the desire to tell others. One of the reasons Simon Peter was such an effective preacher at Pentecost was that it was just a few days after he had tasted the forgiveness of God. It was fresh to him, so he spoke, preached, and taught with a greater sense of urgency and unction, due to his experience. He had just tasted the forgiveness of God. He knew what it was to be forgiven.

One of the problems in churches today, in Sunday school classes and in pulpits, is that it's been too long since people who are teaching the Word of God have tasted the forgiveness of God themselves. If we are to be effective in our testimony, in our witness, in our education, and in our proclamation, then we are going to have to regularly revisit the well of forgiveness. We are going to have to know the fresh touch of His grace and mercy.

The fact is, only the forgiven man is fit to teach transgressors the way of the Lord. David knows about what he's going to be teaching. A man cannot teach what he does not know. Someone who is computer illiterate cannot teach a class on computer skills. A man can't lead somewhere he has never been. A tour guide can't lead a group of people, for example, on a pilgrimage to the Holy Land if he has never been there before. If he has not seen it, not known about it, and not studied about it, then he needs to be led. He certainly should not be leading, because he just may lead others astray. There is nothing more frightening than to see the blind leading the blind.

TO THE TRANSGRESSORS

King David had been taught in a school of experience. The best teachers are those who teach from personal experience, so David says, "Then I will teach."

Who will he teach though? He answers, "Then I will teach transgressors." Look at his audience. David's heart is heavy for transgressors. That's his target audience. That's who he's interested in teaching. If he couldn't edify the saints, he could certainly teach the sinners. He would be speaking from personal experience to people who were caught in the death throes of sin, just like he once was.

In some churches people have gathered in their own groups for so long that they can hardly remember a time when someone came to grace afresh. In some churches, it has been so long since anyone has been newly converted and has been forgiven that the congregation has all but forgotten about the power of the gospel. For some believers, it has been so long since they have tasted the forgiveness of God themselves, that there's little dynamic in their witness, their teaching, or their preaching.

It is a great help when counseling a person, to be able to say, "I know what you're going through. I've been there." There's nothing like personal experience. David said, "Then I'll teach transgressors." He openly—even notoriously—acknowledged his transgressions. Who better to teach transgressors but a forgiven transgressor. There's just something about someone who's been there. There's nothing like personal experience.

ONE WAY

But, what would David propose to teach these transgressors? He says, "Then I will teach transgressors Your ways." The ways of God. That Hebrew word literally means "your road," "your path," "your journey." David will offer the lost a map. He will provide them with emergency road service. And the result of this teaching? He says, "Sinners shall be converted to You." Once they know the way, those transgressors will return to God.

What is the result of finding the forgiveness of God? It has been a long time since many of us have tasted it. We have harbored resentments and never asked God to forgive us for it. We have had broken fellowship with other believers in Christ and never asked God to forgive us for it. But once we do ask for forgiveness, what is the result? We'll have a life dedicated to teaching transgressors, to using our own life experiences for good. We will have the providential opportunity to use our moral earthquakes as a part of our testimony for God's glory. We will be able to take the tragic circumstances of our failures and foibles and use them to minister to others. To what end? So that folks might know God's way. And, ultimately, so that sinners might be converted to Him.

EXALTATION

The fruit of forgiveness includes a new dedication to education. But, it also includes a new dedication to exaltation. Thus, David prays: "Deliver me from the guilt of bloodshed, O God, the God of my salvation, and my tongue shall sing aloud of Your righteousness. O Lord, open my lips, and my mouth shall show forth Your praise (Ps. 51:14–15).

King David says, "If God forgave me—and He did—then I will surely sing and I will praise His name." I will praise. That word literally means "a song" or "a hymn of praise." Only the man or woman who knows the forgiveness of God has a song in their heart. Those who don't know the forgiveness of God just go through the motions. They may come into corporate worship, mouth some words, and make some noise, but they don't sing from their hearts.

David's lips had been sealed for a year. He was in a barren foreign land of the soul. He was wandering in the parched desert land of Nod. The children of Israel, when down in Babylon, asked, "How can we sing the Lord's song in a foreign land?" and they hung their harps on the willow trees.

There are a lot of folks like that. David couldn't sing for all those months. He had no song. He refused to admit that he had done anything wrong. His lips had been sealed by shame. He knew that if he sang praises to the Lord, those in that inner circle who really knew would know what a hypocrite he actually was. But after his prayer of confession and repentance, a song began to well up in his heart. His first reaction, after wanting to teach others, was to sing praises to God. This had once been his very life. From the shepherd's fields outside Bethlehem to the anguished royal courts of King Saul, he would take his harp and sing songs of praise. This was the heart of the legacy he ultimately left, exemplified in the Psalms. No one knew the songs of praise more than David.

Note that he says he will sing of the righteousness of God. One would expect him to sing of God's mercy, but no; he says he will sing of God's righteousness. He realized that God's mercy was only possible through the righteous demands of the law being met.

So, what happens to a man when he finds the forgiveness of God? First he wants to teach transgressors God's ways. Then his life becomes a testimony and sacrifice of praise. And where does that lead? It leads to a life dedicated to exhortation.

EXHORTATION

The final fruit of forgiveness takes the form of an exhortation. The sacrifice King David had to bring before the Lord was a broken and a crushed spirit. This is indeed an exhortation to us.

What does the Lord desire from us? Our sacrifices? Our service? No, he wants us—a broken heart and a broken and contrite spirit. He doesn't want gifts. He wants the giver.

David closes his great prayer of confession and repentance, saying: "Do good in Your good pleasure to Zion. Build the walls of Jerusalem. Then You shall be pleased with the sacrifices of righteousness, with burnt offering and whole burnt offering; then they shall offer bulls on Your altar" (Ps. 51:18–1).

One might say, "Hmmm, is that a contradiction? Didn't he just say, God didn't want sacrifices?"

Indeed, David asserts, "You do not delight in burnt offerings, or else I'd give it to you." But there is no contradiction at all. What King David asked for Jerusalem, we should ask for the church. What God did for King David, God will do for any and all of us—forgive us, make us healthy spiritually, and make us happy and whole.

There's a sense in which King David looks forward here to a millennial city. He anticipates the dawn of a new day, when repentant Israel will find safety in the Lord Jesus Himself. Thus, he says, "Then you shall be pleased with the sacrifices of righteousness, with burnt offerings and whole burnt offerings." The restoration of the levitical sacrifices in the millennial reign of Christ—offered again on the temple mount—will not be intended to merit salvation. Calvary took care of that once and for all. They will be a memorial—like the Lord's Supper is to us—so that His redeemed people will never forget that supreme sacrifice. They will be resurrected in that day to memorialize the great sacrifice of the Lamb of God. They will memorialize the great cost of Calvary.

Thus, we can indeed pray with fervor, "Do good in Your good pleasure to Zion."

When we get right with God, our energy and our prayers move past our own selfish interests and are directed to the entire family of faith. And when we are cleansed and restored with the joy of salvation, that will be our prayer, "Do good to Zion, by your own good pleasure." It will be our greatest pleasure to edify the body of Christ.

The fact is, it is more important what you are when you pray than it is what you pray. And thus, the greatest of the fruits of forgiveness is the fact that God makes us anew. He makes us new creations. He enables us to be what we are supposed to be, so that we can, in turn, do what we are supposed to do.

Moral Soundings

- Is there evidence of the Spirit's indwelling in your life?
- Do you still experience the joy in your relationship with God?
- Do you attempt to make deals with God?
- Do you counsel others who have had similar trials and struggles as you?

Part Four:

RESTORING THE FOUNDATIONS: RECLAIMING LOST GROUND

I was sinking deep in sin,
far from the peaceful shore,
Very deeply stained within,
sinking to rise no more;
But the Master of the sea
heard my despairing cry,
From the waters lifted me,
now safe am I.

—James Rowe

–13–

RESCUE EFFORTS

*Two are better than one. If one falls down,
his friend is there to pick him up. But pity the man that falls
and has no one to help him up.*
Ecclesiastes 4:9–10

ᢒᕒ

If a person suffers a moral earthquake, if they crumble under the pressures of temptation, if their faults cause their downfall, what are we to do? Especially if this person is a Christian brother or sister, how are we to react? What is our role? Indeed, are we to do anything?

It is not a particularly comfortable subject for any of us to discuss, but we simply must talk about the subject of picking up the pieces of broken lives—the ministry of restoration. Certainly, it is not a subject the Bible avoids. For instance, the apostle Paul forthrightly asserts: "Brethren, if a man is overtaken in any trespass, you who are spiritual restore such a one in a spirit of gentleness, considering yourself lest you also be tempted. Bear one another's burdens, and so fulfill the law of Christ" (Gal. 6:1–2).

This may well be one of the most important lessons of all in the realm of temptation for the church of Jesus Christ: What do we do when someone falls and falters? We, the members of the body of Christ, must restore that brother or sister.

Now what do you think would happen if a church began to be known as a place of true restoration? If it became a place where those who are down could get up, a place where those who are out could get back in, not a place of condemnation but of confirmation, a place of new beginnings? I will tell you what would happen: Men and women from all over—men and women with wounded hearts and hopes—would flock to such a church to find hope and to find healing. This is the church we find in the New Testament.

Sadly, many Christians are not active in the ministry of restoration. More sadly still, not many churches are involved in the ministry of restoration. In the Body of Christ we have a responsibility to one another. Paul tells us that the responsibility we have to one another is threefold. We should hunt him up, help him up, and hold him up.

HUNTING, HELPING, AND HOLDING

"Brethren, if any man is overcome in a trespass, you who are spiritual hunt him up." Go to him, restore him, take the initiative. Most of us wait for our wounded, fallen friends to come crawling back, saying, "I'm sorry." But so often, the guilt and the shame that comes in being overcome by temptation prevent one from doing that very thing. In fact, a lot of people are not in church today simply because they're afraid of rejection. They've been overtaken in a trespass, and the fear is that if they should come back to church, they would be rejected!

The ministry of restoration, to the believer, involves hunting him up—seeking him out. We have to go to him; he won't come to us.

Secondly, we are to help him up. Paul says, "Restore him." Our responsibility does not end in seeking out our fallen friends, but in restoring them. And then that's not enough. We're not to stop there. We are to hold them up. Paul admonishes us, "Bear one another's burdens and so fulfill the law of Christ." And the law of Christ is the law of love.

Now what do we do when we find a fallen friend? When dealing with temptation, it's not enough just to talk about everything that precedes the fall, yet sometimes that's what we do in the church of Jesus Christ. We're good about how to overcome temptation, how to spot it, how to stop it, but what do we do when someone falls? We are to hunt them up. By and large, in our generation, we have not been very good at this.

We're better at writing him off and then saying to one another, "I told you so." We like to wait for that fallen one to come back to us, but the Scripture is explicit. It says that our position is to hunt him up, to be the initiator, and to go to him. Don't wait for him to hunt you up for help. It's not going to happen. Many of us with good intentions have seen a friend, overtaken in a trespass, in a sin, and have just been waiting for them to come back, just been waiting for them to repent, to be restored, to come back—perhaps crawling—to us. It's not going to happen.

Why? Many will not return because of guilt—the shame that sin brings; for others, it is the fear of rejection. We are to take the initiative.

Now the issue: this is a family matter. This isn't talking about going to the lost. Paul issues this admonition to the brethren. The Greek word literally means "of the same womb." Paul is directing us to take proactive measures to protect our fellow family of faith members, those who may have succumbed to temptation and to sin.

When are we to engage in this ministry of restoration? Paul says, "If a man is overtaken in any trespass." That word "overtaken" is very interesting in the Greek. It literally means "caught in the act." It conveys a certain element of surprise. If a man is overtaken—to his surprise—in a trespass, then we are to restore him.

So here is a person who is caught, and he falls. Those little secret faults have been running through his life. He didn't think there was anything to them; he thought he was all right; he thought he'd get away with it. Now, all of a sudden, a moral earthquake has struck.

Paul says, if a brother has been overtaken in a trespass in this way, then there is something for us to do. We are to hunt him up and seek to restore him. He could get hurt if he stays out there, outside the boundary lines of God's Word. All of us are susceptible to being overcome by trespasses, even the great men of faith in the Bible: Moses, Elijah, and David.

One day, David stepped over the line, trespassed outside the boundary lines of the Word of God. Yet he was fortunate enough to have a friend named Nathan who hunted him up, helped him up, held him up, confronted him in a spirit of gentleness, and said, "You're that man." We read Psalm 51 and see the repentant heart of David, how that friend of his helped him and held him up.

Paul wrote the Galatian epistle at the end of his first missionary journey. Remember what happened on that first missionary journey? There was a young man by the name of John Mark. He accompanied Paul and Barnabas and then went AWOL. He quit. He gave up. He left them in the lurch, and went back home.

How was John Mark restored? Barnabas was his friend, and what did Barnabas do? He hunted John Mark up. Being a spiritual man, he hunted Mark up and helped him up; he restored him. Then he held him up, he stood by him, and he encouraged him. John Mark went on to leave us that Gospel that bears his name— the Gospel of Mark.

Why? Because Mark had a friend who—when he got outside the boundary lines and was overtaken in a trespass—sought him out and restored him. Barnabas didn't wait for John Mark to come crawling back, saying, "I'm sorry." He went out and, in a spirit of gentleness, hunted him up, helped him up, held him up, and God gave him another opportunity.

THE SPIRITUAL

Not everyone in the church of Jesus Christ is supposed to be involved in the ministry of restoration. Paul says the initiator in this ministry of restoration must be uniquely qualified: "You who are spiritual." The reason is simple: carnal people, those who are not spiritual, will do more damage than they will help.

The call is issued to "you who are spiritual," not you who are holier-than-thou. This is not open season for church people to think it's their God-given call to go out to everybody overtaken in a trespass and confront them, seeking to be part of the ministry of restoration. It is only for those who are spiritual, not self-righteous, not holier-than-thou.

This Greek word for "spiritual" here literally means "one who is filled with and governed by the Holy Spirit." The call to restoration is not to be heeded by everyone. Only those who are spiritual need apply for this job.

Earlier in his Galatian letter, Paul defined just who "the spiritual" were. They were those whose lives genuinely evidence the fruit of the Spirit. He says: "The fruit of the Spirit is love, joy, peace, longsuffering, kindness, goodness, faithfulness, gentleness, self-control. Against such there is no law. And those who are Christ's have crucified the flesh with its passions and desires. If we live in the Spirit, let us also walk in the Spirit. Let us not become conceited, provoking one another, envying one another. Brethren, if a man is overtaken in a trespass, you who are spiritual restore such a one" (Gal. 5:22–6:1).

The one who is spiritual reacts with genuine concern and genuine remorse. He is aware that if this is a true brother who is wounded, he's wounded too. They're members of the same family. They are parts of the same body, and if a part of his body is hurting, he's hurting too. Those who are spiritual realize that. The church must get past the false assumption that the one who has fallen is the one who needs to be the initiator of restoration.

TAKING THE NEXT STEP

Pursuit—even loving pursuit—of our fallen brother is not enough. We must take the process of restoration to the next step. What are we to do? We're to hunt him up, yes, but we're also to help him up.

The word for "restore" literally means "to mend something that is broken or that is torn." It is used in the Gospels to describe nets that were in need of repair. It is also used to describe a broken bone, one in need of mending. The word-picture portrays the idea of putting a bone back in place so that it mends and is useful again, or fixing rends in a net so that it can be used to fish again.

In the ministry of reconciliation and restoration, God uses us to mend that which is torn and to heal that which is broken. He wants to use us, those of us who are spiritual. He wants to use us as His orthopedic physicians to set the broken bones of our time in place so that He can do His own work of healing. He wants to use us to do that, those of us whose lives are characterized by love, joy, peace, gentleness, faithfulness, and self-control. God wants us to be His fixer-uppers.

Here is a man, and the secret faults in his life have erupted into a moral earthquake. Instead of talking about him or lamenting the fact that it's done, we are to go to him, restore him, help him to set those things in place in a spirit of gentleness, so that God can bring hope and healing. The sad commentary with a lot of believers today is that instead of going to a broken brother, they go to others and talk about him.

I SPY

Some like to criticize, some like to condemn, some like to castigate, others like to critique, and some like to cancel—just forget the offending parties. Some say, "It's none of my business. He made his bed, let him lie in it!" But the Bible says, "Brethren, if a man is overtaken in a trespass, you who are spiritual, put that bone in place, mend that torn net."

George W. Truett once said, "I think nothing of that system of espionage which is forever spying out people to catch up with their weaknesses and their faults."

Some churches are into spy activities. There is no place in the church of Jesus Christ for brothers and sisters lying in wait, spying on one another in a spirit of espionage to bring down instead of to build up, to tear down instead of holding up. Our business is to restore. Too many times the very place that God has ordained to be the center of restoration—the church of Jesus Christ—has become the center of condemnation. That's why so many churches are empty today. Instead of being the very center of the place of restoration where wounded broken lives can come, be set together, and become whole, they become places of condemnation.

God uses us as agents of restoration. What are we to do? We're to hunt them up, and we're to help them up.

Imagine going out during the noon hour in a metropolitan area when the streets are filled with people—pedestrians walking everywhere—and seeing a lady step off of a curb. She trips and breaks her arm. Lying there in the street, she is writhing in pain.

One person walks by and says to his friend, "Look at her lying there. She's broken her arm." Another sees her lying there in pain and simply criticizes her, "You're in the way of pedestrian traffic. We're trying to get by here, and we have to step over you. Can't you move?" Someone else stops, but only to counsel the woman. "You know, if you had watched where you were going you wouldn't have tripped over that curb." Now she really needs to hear that, doesn't she? Someone else looks on from a distance and condemns the poor woman. "That's stupid. That is so stupid. She shouldn't have done that."

Sound ridiculous? Certainly it does! And yet, that is precisely how we act when we find that a brother or a sister has been caught in a trespass.

Just because that lady has broken her arm does not mean it must be amputated. It can be mended. It can be put back in place. It can be restored, and it can become useful again.

Why is the church of Jesus Christ hobbling through this world, limping and struggling along in many places? Because there are a lot of broken bones in the body of Christ that have never been properly set. The thrust of the word *restore* is in getting the wrong-doer back to where he should be. It is in getting the bones back in place so that they can be mended and become useful again. It is in getting the nets mended so they can be useful again. It is in getting fallen Christians restored to usefulness, just as strong as ever.

I wonder how many broken bones there are in the body of Christ today? How many wounded lives are there? If a broken bone is not set properly, it may never heal the way it should, and the longer it waits to get set, the longer it gets set in it's own way—deformed. If the believer is not restored, the strength of the church is weakened.

We are members of the same family. We are soldiers in the same army. We are bones, as it were, in the same body. We are all a part of the same net, and when there is a tear in the net, it ceases to be effective. When a part of that net is ripped and torn, fish get out.

We need to realize our world is hurting and broken, and, "brethren, if a man is overtaken in a trespass, you who are spiritual restore [him] in a spirit of gentleness, considering yourself, lest you also be tempted. Bear one another's burdens, and so fulfill the law of Christ" (Gal. 6:1–2).

Set those broken bones so they can walk again. Mend those torn nets so they can fish again. Restore those fallen lives so they can live again. That's what we're to do. We're to hunt them up and help them up and hold them up. This vision of a place of restoration, with us acting as agents of restoration, should be the goal of our churches. Only through application of these principles can we hope to restore the aftereffects of a moral earthquake.

Moral Soundings

- Have you ever sought out the broken and fallen in your midst?
- Have you ever followed the "hunt up, help up, and hold up" pattern?
- Have you ever been pursued by a faithful friend who simply wouldn't let go when you fell?
- Have you ever been used by God to mend or heal or restore?

THE CALL TO RESTORATION

So then, my beloved, just as you have always obeyed, not as in my presence only, but now much more in my absence, work out your salvation with fear and trembling.
Philippians 2:12, NASB

પ્

In the aftermath of a great natural disaster like an earthquake, a tremendous amount of labor must be exerted. Things cannot simply be left alone. The devastation and destruction cannot be ignored. The mess won't go away if we simply ignore it long enough.

So, everyone has to pitch in, work together, and labor side by side. The entire community must be mobilized. Otherwise, the work will never get done, and life will never get back to anything resembling normalcy.

Similarly, the clean-up effort following a moral earthquake can be an enormous undertaking. Yet however difficult, however unpleasant, and however unnerving, it must be done. And it must be done in cooperation with others. It requires a group effort. The entire community of faith must be mobilized.

Like a severely ill patient, a fallen man cannot and will not be able to heal himself. Most fallen Christians hide from the healing, yet revealing, touch of God. Therefore, they must be sought out by their brethren. Once found, they must be helped up from their fallen, decaying state. Then, after this lifting up has been accomplished, they must be held up, much like a baby trying to walk or a patient trying to recover. The fallen brother needs support and encouragement from those around him. From this point on, there exists more responsibility on the part of the patient. Indeed, more active effort is required from them to bring them back to their former strength and role.

THE PROCESS OF RESTORATION

As we discussed in the previous chapter, there are three things the apostle Paul admonishes us as believers in Christ to do with our fallen friends. Hunt them up. Help them up. And hold them up. He says: "Brethren, if a man is overtaken in any trespass, you who are spiritual restore such a one in a spirit of gentleness, considering yourself, lest you also be tempted. Bear one another's burdens, and so fulfill the law of Christ" (Gal. 6:1–2).

It is always a good habit in Bible study to ask ourselves several questions: When? Who? What? How? and Why? When we do this, it is utterly amazing how beautifully and clearly Scripture unfolds for us.

So in this passage, we ask: When? The answer: When one is overtaken in a trespass. Who? You who are spiritual. What? Restore him. How? In a spirit of gentleness. Why? Considering yourself lest you also be tempted.

By asking those simple questions, a wealth of truth emerges from this passage of God's Word. We are to hunt up those who have fallen, but we are to simultaneously help him up. And we are to do it all in a spirit of gentleness, meekness, and humility—remembering from whence we have come ourselves.

The word translated "gentleness," in the Greek text literally means "an animal that has been completely tamed—domesticated." It describes a wild stallion that some cowboy has broken. It's no longer wild. It no longer bucks. The cowboy can get on the back of that horse, flick the reigns a little bit to the left, and the horse, will turn to the left; a little to the right and it'll turn right. He can pull back slightly and it'll stop. That wild stallion has come under the control of his master. That is the word-picture that the apostle Paul uses to describe the kind of spirit we are to display in the process of restoration: it is a spirit of gentleness.

In other words, our obedience to restore our fallen brethren must be conducted in love. We must speak the truth in love, having come under the control of our Master.

THE LOVE CONNECTION

Jesus said, "If you love Me, you will keep My commandments" (John 14:15, NASB). And again, He said: "He who has My commandments and keeps them, he it is who loves Me; and he who loves Me shall be loved by My father, and I will love him, and will disclose Myself to him" (John 14:21, NASB).

Similarly, the apostle John wrote:

> By this we know that we have come to know Him, if we keep His commandments. The one who says, "I have come to know Him," and does not keep His commandments, is a liar, and the truth is not in him; but whoever keeps His word, in him the love of God has truly been perfected. By this we know that we are in Him: the one who says he abides in Him ought himself to walk in the same manner as He walked. Beloved, I am not writing a new commandment to you, but an old commandment which you have had from the beginning; the old commandment is the word which you have heard. (1 John 2:3–7, NASB)

The unmistakable mark of a faithful people is obedience. Believers are proved as "doers of the word, and not merely hearers who delude themselves" (James 1:22, NASB). They keep the commands of God's Word.

Thus James could ask:

> What use is it, my brethren, if a man says he has faith, but he has no works? Can that faith save him? If a brother or sister is without clothing and in need of daily food, and one of you says to them, "Go in peace, be warmed and be filled," and yet you do not give them what is necessary for their body, what use is that? Even so faith, if it has no works, is dead, being by itself. But someone may

well say, "You have faith, and I have works; show me your faith without the works, and I will show you my faith by my works." (James 2:14–18, NASB)

Regardless of what anyone else does or says, we have a responsibility to obey God. Every believer has an irrevocable duty to demonstrate the authenticity of their faith. Each of us is called to keep Christ's commandment to show compassion and care for the hurting and for the fallen.

There is simply no getting around it. We can make excuses all day long, but they won't change the fact that we are obligated by our faith in the Lord Jesus to do right. Everyone else around us may be sidetracked by theological side issues or evangelical sideshows, but we still have no "outs." We have a job to do. We must "keep His commandments."

Yet our obedience must not be a dry, lifeless compliance to the letter of the law. Our righteousness must surpass that of the scribes and the Pharisees (see Matt. 5:20). Our righteousness must be marked by love. Our obedience is to be a joyous exercise of lovingkindness (Ps. 109:16).

Just as our obedience is evidence that our love for God is authentic, so our love for those around us is evidence that our obedience is authentic.

Once again, the apostle of obedience and love, John, asserts: "We know that we have passed out of death into life, because we love the brethren. He who does not love abides in death" (1 John 3:14, NASB).

Again he says: "We know love by this, that He laid down His life for us; and we ought to lay down our lives for the brethren. But whoever has the world's goods, and beholds his brother in need and closes his heart against him, how does the love of God abide in him? Little children, let us not love with word or with tongue, but in deed and truth. We shall know by this that we are of the truth, and shall assure our heart before Him" (1 John 3:16–19, NASB).

When asked by the scribes, "'What commandment is the foremost of all?' Jesus answered: 'The foremost is, "Hear, O Israel;

The Lord our God is one Lord; and you shall love the Lord your God with all your heart, and with all your soul, and with all your mind, and with all your strength." The second is this, 'You shall love your neighbor as yourself.' There is no other commandment greater than these'" (Mark 12:28–31, NASB).

Our love of God is shown by obedience. Our obedience is shown by love of man. It is an endless cycle. It is a marvelous cycle that makes faith in Christ not just right, and not just true, but abundantly satisfying as well (see John 10:7–18).

THE PATH OF LOVE

Sadly, *love* is an overused, much abused word in our everyday vocabularies. When we say that we "love" Mom, hot dogs, apple pie, and baseball, we reduce the word's impact terribly. When "love" can mean one thing to a Hollywood starlet, another to a Madison Avenue ad man, another to a gay activist on Castro Street in San Francisco, another to an Arab terrorist for Gadhafi or Khomeini's Jihad, and still another to the man on the street, "love" ceases to mean much at all. In fact, a word that can mean almost anything to anybody will soon come to mean almost nothing to everybody. But, even though our culture may be a bit muddy in its understanding of "love", the Bible is absolutely clear:

> Love is patient, love is kind, and is not jealous; love does not brag and is not arrogant, does not act unbecomingly; it does not seek its own, is not provoked, does not take into account a wrong suffered, does not rejoice in unrighteousness, but rejoices with the truth; bears all things, believes all things, hopes all things, endures all things. Love never fails; but if there are gifts of prophecy, they will be done away; if there are tongues, they will cease; if there is knowledge, it will be done away. (1 Cor. 13:4–8, NASB)

Love involves "compassion, kindness, humility, gentleness, and patience" (Col. 3:12–14). It involves single-mindedness (see Phil. 2:2). It involves purity of heart, a good conscience, and "a faith unfeigned" (1 Tim. 1:5, KJV). It involves diligence (see 2 Cor. 8:7), knowledge (see Phil. 1:9), service (see Gal. 5:13), righteousness (see 2 Tim. 2:22), sound judgment (see Phil. 1:9), and courtesy (see 1 Pet. 3:8). Love is the royal law (see James 2:8). It is the capstone of godly character (see 1 Cor. 13:13). It is the message that we have heard from the beginning (see 1 John 3:11).

Interestingly, the word that the King James translators chose to use in each of these passages was "charity." That word catches a special dynamic of meaning that "love" has lost in our day of muddy definitions. "Charity" accurately communicates the fact that love is not simply a feeling. Love is something you do. Love is an action. Love is a commitment, an obligation, and a responsibility. Love is charity.

Thus, we are to prove the sincerity of love (see 2 Cor. 8:8, KJV), and we are to do it by following "after charity" (1 Cor. 14:1), by having "fervent charity" among ourselves (1 Pet. 4:8, KJV), and by being an example to others "in charity" (1 Tim. 4:12, KJV). For "charity shall cover the multitude of sins" (1 Pet. 4:8, KJV). "Though I speak with the tongues of men and of angels, and have not charity, I am become as sounding brass, or a tinkling cymbal. And though I have the gift of prophecy, and understand all mysteries, and all knowledge; and though I have all faith, so that I could remove mountains, and have not charity, I am nothing. And though I bestow all goods to feed the poor, and though I give my body to be burned, and have not charity, it profiteth me nothing" (1 Cor. 13:1–3, KJV).

There is simply no getting around it. It is a Christian necessity to do the work of charity among those who are hurting or fallen, to love not just "in word or in tongue, but in deed and in truth" (1 John 3:18).

Even if no one else cares. Even if no one else helps. Even if no one else tries, we must.

THE LOVE OF JESUS

Restoration is thus to be undertaken in an environment of lovingkindness and gentleness. If someone has a broken bone, you don't approach him with a sledgehammer. This is why those who are not spiritual have no place in the ministry of restoration. Those who are spiritual, have to handle broken people firmly, but gently. A broken man needs compassion. He needs someone in a spirit of love and gentleness.

What made Jesus Christ so winsome? There were times when people were convicted of their sin just by being around him, and yet the crowds flocked to Him and followed Him. What was it about Him that was so winsome?

He was a man of compassion. He never spoke a harsh or unkind word to a broken man or woman. He certainly pulled no punches with the hard-hearted—the vipers and snakes, the whitewashed tombs and hypocrites. But He met in compassion those who were broken, those who needed restoration, and those who were fallen. Those who were overtaken in a trespass, He didn't criticize. He didn't condemn them. He didn't castigate them. He was in the restoration business, and the more you become like Jesus Christ, the more you will take on that spirit of love and gentleness.

EXTREMISM

Most of us float to one of two extremes. Most churches, most Christians, go from pillar to post. On the one hand we have the condemners—the extreme fundamentalists and legalists. On the other extreme are the condoners—the extreme liberals and libertines. One condemns just about anything and everything; the other condones just about anything and everything.

The condemners represent the pharisaical extreme. That is, they are morally upright; but they are stern, unkind, and unforgiving. Their holier-than-thou attitudes drive those who have fallen even farther away, deeper into sin. This is a group who condemns trespasses.

The condoners represent the herodian extreme, like those Jews who compromised with Herod in Jesus' day. They are permissive to the point of being promiscuous. The condoners have no real moral standards. They may talk about principles here or there, but they really don't believe that there are any absolutes. Everyone does what they like. No one says anything. Everyone finds unconditional acceptance lest someone accuse the church of judgment or intolerance. They don't condemn sin. They go to the opposite extreme. They condone it. Even by their silence, they condone it. And they put the Word of God and its standards for holiness, righteousness, and morality aside.

But genuine biblical restoration can be found in neither one of these extremes. Instead, it is to be found in the admonition set forth by Paul: the wrongdoing is not to be condemned and it is not to be condoned. It is to be confronted. By whom? By those who are spiritual. How? In a spirit of gentleness. Why? That we might restore the fallen one to fellowship in the church and with the family of God.

There are a lot of hurting, broken people around us. Thus, it is vital that we avoid the extremes and simply do the important work of building bridges of reconciliation and restoration. But how do we go about doing this?

BEARING BURDENS

According to the apostle Paul, the fulfillment of our calling to obey Christ's commands in a loving and gentle fashion may be accomplished when we simply bear one another's burdens: "Bear one another's burdens and so fulfill the law of Christ." (Gal. 6:1).

We need to go above and beyond the ordinary in order to win back our fallen brother. It's not enough just to hunt him up and to help him up. We must also hold him up, and sometimes that means bearing one another's burdens, to fulfill the law of Christ.

The New Testament is replete with stories of men and women who were down but who got up, who found this principle of restoration to be true. For instance, there was the woman in Sycar at a well one day. What happened? Jesus put into practice the ministry of restoration. First, He hunted her up. He went way out of His way. Remember? He said He needed to go through Samaria. He went miles out of His way. Why? To hunt up that one woman. Then, He helped her up. He told her of living water. Next, He held her up—she went into Sycar, and she brought her whole village out to meet Him.

What about Simon Peter when he betrayed Christ? He blew it. He fell ignobly. He wept bitterly. What did Jesus do? He arose from the grave, and He hunted him up. He appeared first unto Simon, and then unto the disciples. Somewhere, after the Resurrection, Jesus found Simon Peter and allowed him to weep out those tears of repentance. He hunted him up, He helped him up, and He held him up.

Think of Thomas: "Except I see those prints in his hands, I'll not believe." And what did Jesus do? He hunted him up. He came back to the Upper Room where Thomas was and came through the door. Hunted him up, and then helped him up. He said to Thomas, "Here they are, put your finger in here." Then He held him up. Thomas eventually took the gospel of Christ all the way to India and later died a martyr's death.

Yes, we're to hold up the fallen brother. We are to bear his burdens, and so fulfill the law of Christ.

PERSONAL RESPONSIBILITY

Again, we must remember the responsibility that each of us has concerning our salvation, whether we are recovering or walking strong: We must work out our salvation with fear and trembling. We are responsible to God for seeking to eliminate those faults, those cracks which cause us to crumble, which cause moral earthquakes. We must remember that any brother being restored must desire to be restored. He must be repentant.

Just because we hunt him up and help him up does not mean restoration takes place. I've had experiences in my own life with preacher friends and laymen friends that I've hunted up when they were taken in trespasses—people I've sought to help. There are times when we hunt up people, but they will not let us help them up nor hold them up. The broken one has to be willing to repent. The fallen one overtaken in a trespass must yield to the Holy Spirit, be willing to repent, and if need be, make reconciliation, restitution, or whatever else may be involved. If he will not repent, there is no restoration.

Someone once asked, "When can a brother who has fallen into sin be used again?" It's a good question. It's a question that we're confronted with often. When someone God has used before has fallen into sin, when can they be used again? When can they be restored again? What was Spurgeon's reply? "When a man's repentance is as notorious as his sin." When a man's repentance becomes as well known as his sin, when a man's heart of true genuine repentance is as well known as his trespass—he is ready to be used again.

King David, was a great sinner, but God used him again. Why? Because he was a great repenter, and his repentance became as notorious as his sin. Psalm 51 shows how his heart was opened, and he was filled with the spirit of repentance.

Some folks have a false concept of repentance. Repentance means a change of mind. That's what the Greek word means literally, a "change of mind." Some people think repentance is remorse, just being sorry that you committed an infraction of God's standards. But that is wide of the mark. Remember the rich young ruler? He was sorrowful—but he did not repent.

Other people think repentance is regret—wishing we hadn't done it. A lot of us live like that when we've fallen, but that's not repentance either. Remember Pontius Pilate, washing his hands in that basin of water, regretting his deed? But he did not repent.

Still others think repentance is reform—in other words, turning over a new leaf. "I'm just gonna try harder and try better and just reform." But that is not repentance either. Judas Iscariot reformed. He took the thirty pieces of silver, went back, and flung them down the corridors of the temple. He reformed, but he didn't repent.

Repentance means a change of mind. It's when our volition is transformed. It's when our will is changed. If we've truly changed our mind, our volition—our will—is completely altered. And what will happen if our will is changed? Our actions will likewise be changed.

Now we can hunt up folks and help up folks and hold up folks all day long, but if they don't have a genuine spirit of repentance, they'll never be restored. We can help the invalids up, but until they put a foot on the ground, until they make an effort to change themselves, our efforts will be in vain.

We do have one consolation in this regard. As David attests in the Psalms, the pressure of the hand of God is a terrible thing. It will not let up; it continues to push those fallen brothers who anguish over their sin until they repent. But if no one is present, if no one hunts them up, then no one will be there to offer them the much-needed hand of fellowship, the much-needed hand of loving restoration. That would be the greatest tragedy of all.

Moral Soundings

- Have you ever taken seriously the call to seek and restore your fallen brethren?
- Is your love for God expressed in obedience to His Word?
- Is your obedience to His Word expressed in love for God?
- Is your love and obedience expressed in tangible efforts to restore the fallen?

–15–

THE GOD OF THE SECOND CHANCE

If we confess our sins,
He is faithful and just to forgive us our sins
and to cleanse us from all unrighteousness.
1 John 1:9

૱☙

Everyone, at one time or another, has done something which we know offends and disappoints someone whom we respect and love. When we commit such an act, we usually feel hesitant about seeing that person again, even though a visit with them is probably what is most necessary to heal the breach. Such a meeting becomes more strongly desired the longer it does not occur. Many times the Holy Spirit presses down on us, yet we will not or cannot take immediate steps to rectify the situation. How much more pleasant it is for us to discover that we are forgiven when the meeting finally takes place. When we are restored to our Christian brothers and sisters, it tastes sweet to our spirit. Following Christ's resurrection, we see the occurrence of just that sort of restoration—one in which the parties have been separated and unable to resolve it before now:

> When the Sabbath was over, Mary Magdalene, Mary the mother of James, and Salome bought spices so that they might go to anoint Jesus' body. Very early on the first day of the week, just after sunrise, they were on their way to the tomb and they asked each other, "Who will roll the stone away from the entrance of the tomb?" But when they looked up, they saw that the stone, which was very large,

had been rolled away. As they entered the tomb, they saw a young man dressed in a white robe sitting on the right side, and they were alarmed. "Don't be alarmed," he said. "You are looking for Jesus the Nazarene, who was crucified. He has risen! He is not here. See the place where they laid him. But go, tell his disciples and Peter, 'He is going ahead of you into Galilee. There you will see him, just as he told you.'" (Mark 16:1–7, NIV)

In this text are two words that make all the difference in life. When grasped and applied to our own lives, they can make all the difference. The women had come to the tomb to anoint the corpse of our Lord Jesus of Nazareth with spices. When they got there, an angelic being appeared to them, and said, "Don't be afraid. I know why you're here. You're looking for Jesus." Then the angel gave them a message, "Go and tell His disciples and Peter that He is gone before you into Galilee."

UPON THIS ROCK

The two words that make all the difference are: "and Peter."

Why would those words be inserted here? The angelic being said to go and tell the disciples. Then he paused and added, "And, especially, Jesus wants Peter to know that He's alive, that He's gone to meet *him*, and He's gone before you into Galilee." Why are those words there? Had we been instructing the angel in what to say, we would have probably picked words of antagonism: "Go and tell the disciples and Pontius Pilate." We probably would have gotten a kick out of taunting that Roman procurator who sentenced Christ and then tried to wash his hands of responsibility in the matter. Or, "Go and tell the disciples and King Herod." Or, perhaps, "Go and tell the disciples and Caiaphus." But no, no words of antagonism were spoken here.

Or, if we had been instructing the angel, we might have commissioned him to use words of appreciation. "Go and tell the disciples and John." He was so faithful. He stood there at the cross when the rest of them had gone. He stood there by Mary. Or, "Go and tell the disciples and Nathaniel." Tell the one who was without guile. Or, "Go and tell the disciples and Joseph of Arimathea and Nicodemus." Tell those who so tenderly took the body of Christ from the cross and made arrangements for His burial. But no, they were not words of antagonism or appreciation. Instead, they were words of affection. "Go and tell the disciples and Peter."

Why Peter? The Lord Jesus knew Peter's heart. It was Peter, of course, who had denied the Lord. It was Simon Peter that night who, when Jesus was instructing them of his ensuing death, said, "Even though all these men may turn on You, You can count on me. When the chips are down I'll not desert you. I will not deny you. I'll be there." And across the fire that night Jesus said, "Simon, before that rooster crows, you will have denied Me three times."

Jesus was arrested in Gethsemane's garden, and yes, all the other disciples forsook Him and fled; but Simon Peter followed at a distance. Following the torches of the mob that took Jesus from the Garden of Gethsemane down through the Kidron Valley and up the side of the Mount Zion, up to the house of Caiaphas, where He was placed in the dungeon. Peter sat outside and warmed himself by the fire. Later that night, Peter denied Jesus three times. As they were taking Jesus from one trial to another, He passed by that fire. He didn't say anything. The Bible simply says that He looked at Peter. When Peter saw that look, he heard the rooster crow. The Bible says he went out and wept bitterly.

He needed a word of encouragement. The message at the tomb shows us the heart of a loving father toward a child who has made a mistake—a father who believes in the second chance.

THE MESSAGE OF THE TOMB

What is the message of Easter? What is the message of the empty tomb but the message of second chance? Many of us have faced our sorrows and setbacks, just as Peter did. Easter means there is hope. Easter means what we've done before won't matter anymore when we've seen Jesus. It is the message of the new beginning. It is the message of the second chance.

The second chance is possible. Some of us don't believe that. Peter didn't for a while. How do we finally believe? We believe because of the Resurrection. If there were no Resurrection, there would be no gospel, no Good News, and no new beginning.

These two words "And Peter" came like water to a man dying of thirst. Peter thought the Lord would disown him. He had been so brazen and so bold. Then he denied Him and failed so miserably. Talk about good news! When he heard those words, Peter knew that the second chance was possible.

Many people know what it is like to live defeated lives because of something they did or didn't do. The Bible is for them. Page after page, chapter after chapter, book after book, the Bible is the story of men and women who messed up and got a second chance. When it came time to deliver a nation from bondage, who of us would have picked a murderer, one who had been hiding for forty years in virtual obscurity in the desert? Who would have picked Moses to be the emancipator of God's people? God did.

What about David? He was so full of lust for another man's wife that he used his power and prestige to take her, and then tried to cover over his sin by arranging the death of her husband. Who would have said that a man like that could come to be called a man after God's own heart"? God did.

And what about Jonah? This man went in diametric opposition to the will of God for his life. Like many of us who have gone the wrong way, he just kept going down and down, finally into a fish's belly in the depths of the sea. He was regurgitated up onto the shore. Jonah 3:1 says, "Now the word of the Lord came to Jonah the second time, saying, Arise, go to Ninevah.'" And he did. He took advantage of the second chance, and went.

The empty tomb makes possible the second chance. This message of hope is not for those who think they can continue committing the same sin time after time. It is for men and women who, like Simon Peter, have repented, have changed their minds, and wept bitterly. Jesus didn't have a private meeting with Simon Peter because he was a big sinner and because he was guilty. No, it was because he was penitent and sorrowful. It was not his cursing and his denial that brought his mercy. It was his tears and repentance. The Lord is close to the brokenhearted: "The sacrifices of God are a broken spirit, a broken and a contrite heart—These, O God, You will not despise" (Ps. 51:17). "Blessed are the poor in spirit" (Matt. 5:3). There is no hope in the second chance for the one who is simply sorry he or she got caught. It is for one who is truly repentant.

PERSON TO PERSON

The second chance is not only possible, but it is personal. The love of Christ singles us out by name—as individuals. He loves us individually. There is no one else with DNA like yours. No one else with a fingerprint like yours. He knows even the number of hairs on your head: "But the very hairs on your head are all numbered" (Matt. 10:30).

Why does God know so much about us? Because we are individuals. Each person is indescribably valuable to God, and His love comes to us not corporately but individually. He says that He calls His own sheep by name: "The watchman opens the gate for him, and the sheep listen to his voice. He call his own sheep by name and leads them out. I am the good shepherd; I know my sheep and my sheep know me—just as the Father knows me and I know the Father—I have laid down my life for the sheep" (John 10:3–4, 14–15, NIV).

Peter received a personal message on that first Easter Sunday. The angel said to the women, "Go and tell the disciples and Peter." Peter's name, *Petros*, literally means "rock." The message was not, "Go and tell the disciples and Simon." That was his old name. Peter was his new name. When Jesus first saw the fisherman, Andrew, Simon Peter's brother, said, "We have found the

Messiah." He took Simon Peter by the hand and brought him to Jesus. The first time Jesus ever saw Simon Peter, he said, "You are Simon the son of Jonah. You shall be called Cephas, [*Petros*, Peter, a rock]" (John 1:41–42).

Jesus saw potential in Peter. Jesus was saying, one of these days Simon will be called a rock. Jesus also named Peter like a parent proudly names his child as he hopes and dreams for his child's future. He does the same for us. He looks into our lives and He sees us not for who we are but who we could be, what we could become. He sees our future. He sees the potential that is in our lives.

RELIGION V. RELATIONSHIP

Some people know only religion. Christianity is not a religion. Religion, quite honestly, has caused many of the ills of the world throughout the centuries. Christianity is different from all the other world religions. Why? All the other religions focus on man searching for God, man trying to get to God. It is man-centered theology. Christianity is quite the reverse. It is the story of God coming to man clothed in human flesh—Jesus, the Savior of the world.

Christianity is not a religion; it is a relationship. Christ doesn't deal with us in mass, He deals with us individually, and, thus, Christ comes to us.

Peter's fall had been so public. Have you ever been to a children's play when one of the kids suddenly forgets her line? She stands there frozen, while everyone in the audience pulls for that little kid. Those in the audience who know the play desperately mouth the words, trying to help. Or, at a ball game, a little kid is up at bat, and he strikes out. Everyone's heart goes out, wanting to help. I think there's a sense in which all of heaven watched Simon Peter's fall, and now after the Resurrection, it is as though they are all pulling for him to get back up. "Be sure," they said, "to tell Peter that one failure doesn't make a flop. He gets to bat again."

Sin affects our lives so greatly that it is almost completely incomprehensible. Its enduring nature wins over countless attempts by us to subject ourselves to God. It destroys our hearts, our homes, and our plans. It can destroy people completely. In order to defeat so persistent an enemy, we must rely on the strength and power of God, not our own. When facing this greater force, sin must give way. The one thing it cannot do is make God cease loving us. His love prompts God to shower us with his power, forcing the retreat of sin.

This is the heart and soul of the relationship that the Christian faith signifies, celebrates, and exemplifies.

Sin's retreat and defeat is shown again and again in the Bible. When Christ was crucified, sin was rendered powerless over those who had faith in God. Although we falter and fall into sin, its advance is only momentary. God's power has permanently built a bridge between us and Him.

The enemy cannot take that bridge. Sin's power is broken; Satan must content himself with guerrilla raids that, while painful, will ultimately be crushed with him.

At Easter, which marked the defeat of death, a living hope was restored to the people of God. That living hope exists in Christ. Through Him we may be given a second chance—a reconciliation between us and God.

PRIVATE AFFAIRS

The second chance is not only possible and personal, but also private. When Jesus Christ came out of the tomb, the first thing He did was to find Peter. "He was seen by Cephas then by the twelve" (1 Cor. 15:5). Some things are so personal and private that they are not even recorded for us in Scripture. What took place in that remarkable meeting, we may never know. Peter thought he was finished, and the Lord found him privately. We don't know what was said or how things went, but it must have been quite a meeting. We can only imagine the bitter tears, the broken words slowly coming through quivering lips, the deep sobs and long breaks of silence, and the many assurances of Peter's love. How do we know that what we are assuming is true? Because so many of us have actually been there.

What tender consideration we see in our Lord here. He meets Peter alone before ever seeing him with the Twelve. How painful it would have been for Simon Peter to first see the wounds of our Lord in the presence of all those others, publicly. How impossible, with all those others around, to have poured out his love and remorse. Even though Simon Peter denied him publicly, Jesus met him privately—and forgave him privately. It is not enough for us to simply hear the good news that He is risen or to know that the second chance is possible or personal. It comes when we have a private encounter with Jesus Christ.

PROFIT MOTIVE

Finally, the second chance is not only possible, personal, and private, it is also profitable. This meeting transformed Simon Peter. As a result, he became the undisputed, recognized leader of the early church. God's mercy for us drives us to serve Him. We see over and over throughout the Book of Acts Peter, being beaten and imprisoned, saying, "I can't help but speak the things that I've seen and heard." All of this because of two simple and unassuming words, "and Peter."

Those words should speak to all of us. We have a way of remembering our failures and forgetting our strong points. If some church members had been commissioned to give this message, they might have said, "Go and tell the disciples and forget Peter." Remember when Peter was up on the Sea of Galilee and he failed trying to walk on the water? Forget Peter. He denied, he failed. But in the end Simon Peter remained faithful unto death.

In one of his Epistles, Peter wrote, "I think it is right to stir you up by reminding you that shortly I am going to put off this old body, just as Christ has showed me." He was referring to the meeting he had following the Resurrection on the beach in Galilee, when Jesus said, "When you are old, Simon Peter, someone else will stretch out your hands," indicating the death he would die. And, yes, Simon Peter met his own martyr's death through crucifixion. But he didn't count himself worthy to be crucified in tbe same way as our Savior; Peter was crucified, tradition tells us, upside down.

Simon Peter was restored. He was restored fully and completely.

The great American poet Henry Wadsworth Longfellow said that the story of the prodigal is the greatest short story ever written. It is the story about a teenager who found life at home hopelessly boring; Dad was out-of-date and out-of-touch. The boy had heard so many stories of the bright lights of the big city that he decided he was big enough to leave. He went out to the big city and had a great time—for a while. In the end, though, he discovered that the high life is nothing more than hangovers, rip-offs, squandered opportunities, and unemployment lines.

As he was contemplating returning home, he rehearsed a speech that he never got a chance to use. Sitting in a pigpen, eating what the pigs were eating, he said, "I'm going to go home and say to my father that I've sinned and I'm wrong and I'm sorry." He rehearsed that speech over and over. When he went home, the father saw him way down the road and ran off the porch to meet the boy. I once heard my friend Max Lucado describe the scene like this. "There were no pointed fingers, no clenched fists, no crossed arms—not even, 'Where have you been?' or, 'I told you so.'" There was none of that—just open arms. The boy was met with wide, sweet, open arms.

This is the story of the whole Bible. Again and again, the Father welcomes the prodigal home. In fact, the Bible is the book of the second chance.

Look at Jonah: he was down, but he came back. Look at Abraham. He lied about Sarah, but he came back. In the New Testament James even calls him the "friend of God." Look at David. He blew it, but he came back and wrote that wonderful psalm of repentance. Look at Thomas. He doubted, but he came back. Thomas became filled with the Holy Spirit, took the gospel to India, and died a martyr's death. Look at James and John. They were jealous, arguing about which one would have a prominent seat in heaven, but they came back. One of them gained a martyr's death. The other one, as an old man exiled on Patmos, gave us the Apocalypse, the Revelation. Look at John Mark. He quit, but he came back and gave us the Gospel of Mark. And look at Peter. He cursed; he denied; but he came back. After weeping bitterly, he met Jesus in a private meeting and got a second chance. He came back and became the great leader of the New Testament church.

Thank God He can use us even if we mess up. Thank God for a second chance.

Moral Soundings

- How many Biblical examples can you think of that illustrate the second-chance principle?
- Have you appropriated the personal message of the empty tomb?
- Have you accepted the call of God to a private encounter with the living Christ?
- Do you understand the idea that Christianity is not a religion but a relationship?
- Do you actually have such a relationship?

LITTLE IS MUCH

You prepare a table before me
in the presence of my enemies;
you anoint my head with oil;
my cup runs over.
Psalm 23:5

෧෧

In the final analysis, almost every issue seems to be reduced to a question of dollars and cents these days. Whether it is a question of welfare programs or disaster relief, popular entertainment or foreign policy, environmental standards or teen pregnancy rates, educational outcomes or industrial effectiveness—success or failure is invariably measured in financial terms. We want to know what the bottom line is. We want to know how much it is going to cost us. We want to know what kind of return we can expect.

Following each of the earthquakes that have struck California over the past two decades, estimations of impact have invariably been couched in economic terms. It is almost as if the homes, businesses, and even lives lost in such catastrophes can be quantified chiefly as fiscal concerns.

Even moral earthquakes are often analyzed in material terms—revenues lost, alimonies paid, estates divided, and portfolios dissolved. It seems that in our culture today we have accepted as both truth and truism the infamous campaign slogan, "It's the economy, stupid."

The Bible confirms the fact that money matters are important, albeit in a manner entirely different than what our materialistic minds might naturally suppose. Money matters are important from a biblical perspective simply because, according to the Bible, everything in heaven and on earth—every discipline, every issue, and every calling—must come under the authority of the lordship of Jesus Christ.

Many a moral earthquake has been caused by a failure to recognize this fact, and many a recovery from moral disaster has been effected by a righteous appropriation of this fact.

SUPPLY AND DEMAND

If ever there is a subject with wide-ranging dogmatic differences of opinion, it is the economy. Should we balance the budget? Should we stimulate the economy by lowering interest rates? Do we limit supply so prices can remain stable during times of excess?

My undergraduate degree was a Bachelor of Business Administration. During my studies I took a course in elementary economics. In that course, we learned the basic formula of economic function—the law of supply and demand. This law is the entire basis of a free market system. This is what should regulate the prices of all products in the market place. The question is: How does it work?

Very simply stated it is this: when demand exceeds supply, prices go up; when supply exceeds demand, prices go down. Let's say I have a grocery store and I have a bunch of apples in the store. All of a sudden I see about a hundred people lined up outside wanting apples. So what do I do? Before I open the store for the day, I take down that sign that says, "Apples $1," and I put one up that says, "Apples $2." When the people come in, even though the price has been raised, they buy all of the apples anyway. When demand exceeds supply, prices go up.

On the other hand, when supply exceeds demand, prices go down. Here I am at my grocery store with one hundred apples. My store is filled with people, but no one is purchasing apples. In a day or two all the apples are going to rot, and they won't be good for anything. So what do I do? The supply is greater than the demand. Knowing this theory of economics, I go over to the sign that says, "Apples $1," and I replace it with a sign that says, "Apples 25¢." When people pass by, they see it and they buy my apples. Then I can get rid of all my apples. This is the basic the law of supply and demand.

How does this theory apply to us? Discussing basic economic principles in the midst of a study on moral earthquakes may not seem logically related; however, we need to understand how differently God provides for our needs, as opposed to our own ability to supply our needs. For the most part, we are limited to our own financial resources to provide for our needs and our desires. God is only limited by His holy nature. Another problem we have is that we have limited resources. God is not limited by earthly things; He is in control of all of nature. We also have to battle our sinful nature when deciding what our needs are and how to allocate our resources. God knows what we need, and He desires what is best for us.

While some Christians are apologetic about mentioning money—especially when it comes to tithing—I'm not a bit apologetic about it because Jesus spoke so often about it. Thirty-eight parables of our Lord are recorded, and one-third of them deal with our relationship to material possessions. Why? Christ says, "Where your treasure is, that's where your heart will be also." One out of every six verses in the three Synoptic Gospels—Matthew, Mark, and Luke—discuss the proper and righteous use of material goods. Consider for instance:

- Mark 10:25: "It is easier for a camel to go through the eye of a needle than for a rich man to enter the kingdom of God!"

- Matthew 12:35: "A good man out of the good treasure of his heart brings forth good things, and an evil man out of the evil treasure brings forth evil things."

- Luke 19:26: "For I say to you, that to everyone who has will be given; and from him who does not have, even what he has will be taken away from him."

MONEY TALKS

Jesus says in effect, "Your money talks." What does money say about our commitment to Christ? I've often said if I were commissioned to write someone's biography and could have only one thing to use as a reference for that biography, I wouldn't want his family tree nor his prayer journal. I would want his checkbook.

Let's look at the checkbook. It will show us where our heart is. It will show us what things in our lives are most important to us. That's why our wills are so important. A will is called a "last will and testament." It's a testimonial. After we're gone from this earth, it's a testimonial to everybody that's left of what we thought was really important in life.

Our checkbooks may even be an early-warning system for moral earthquakes. Our sinful nature always struggles against wisely allocating our resources; it always clamors for more. We always desire beyond our financial means. We covet. What we desire is immaterial; the important factor is that our desire demonstrates our flawed nature, coveting whatever delights the eye. This problem is made worse by our lifestyles. Most Americans live lives of plenty—all our basic needs are met. Anything beyond those needs is a luxury. We may consider many items necessary that are really luxuries: a television, a microwave, a computer, and even a car. We don't need these things to survive. Yet our sinful desires make us unsatisfied with what we have. The newer, bigger, and better, always exists. Therefore, we desire. Demand exceeds supply; but the Bible clearly states, "The lines have fallen to me in pleasant places; yes, I have a good inheritance"(Ps. 16:6). We will continue to desire until God intervenes.

DEMAND AND SUPPLY

One day our Lord Jesus laid out His economic plan, not in the halls of Congress but on a grassy hillside of a mountain in Galilee. What we see in this remarkable plan ought to startle us all—materialistic as we are. The fact is, without Christ, demand always exceeds supply—and the perpetual cry is: "Not enough!" But with Christ, supply always exceeds demand—and the cry becomes, "More than enough!"

Thus, the prophet Isaiah says: "Come, buy and eat. Yes, come, buy wine and milk without money and without price. Why do you spend money for what is not bread, and your wages for what does not satisfy? Listen carefully to Me and eat what is good, and let your soul delight itself in abundance" (Isa. 55:1–3). When we go to Christ for our needs, we receive satisfying goods in abundance.

If Christ is not factored into the equation of our lives, we will inevitably face deprivation and want. Demand will always exceed supply. For those who try to fill the void of life with money, their cry is, "Not enough!" If we ask them, "How much is enough?" their answer will be, "Just a little more." Why is this? Because when we try to fill the void where Christ belongs with money, we never have enough, and we always think just a little more is enough. Look at our American culture. Look at the number of people declaring bankruptcy because they always wanted more than they could afford. While we seek to feel fulfilled and chase after the America dream, we think that money and things are the means to that end.

That's always the way it is with life. We try to fill the void where Christ belongs with pleasure or with sex, and someone asks us, "How much is enough?" The reply is, "Just a little more."

Now what does this have to do with you and with me? More specifically, what does this have to do with moral earthquakes? Take a look at the story of the feeding of the five thousand, and the relevance becomes obvious.

The demand in that situation was a hungry crowd of five thousand. They came to hear Christ's teachings, and paid no attention to their sustenance needs. The supply was five barley loaves and two small fish—hardly a meal for more than four people. There was definitely a problem with supply and demand.

Three things brought about this problem. First of all, there was no sense of planning. Second, there was no sense of purpose, and, thirdly, there was no sense of potential.

PLANNING, PURPOSE, AND POTENTIAL

Literally thousands of people were out on the Galilean hillside and had not made any preparation for the day. They traveled to the hillside without making any arrangements for their dinner. They didn't think ahead. They had a demand for something of which there was no apparent supply—food, a basic need. Yet, the problem turned into an opportunity for Jesus to work a miracle.

Secondly, there was no sense of purpose. Philip and Andrew, the disciples who brought the problem to the attention of Jesus, had no sense of purpose. They had no idea that they were about to be used that day to the glory of God. When Jesus asked Philip where he was going to buy bread for all these people, he was testing Philip to see what he had in mind as his purpose. The narrative account in the Gospel of John says that Jesus already knew what He was going to do. Christ was testing Philip, calling him to examine himself, saying, "Look at what you are, where you are, and what you are doing. Has it dawned on you that there might be a purpose in your predicament? Has it dawned on you that a demand in your life that's exceeding supply might be there for a reason and a purpose?"

The reason why so many were hungry and without food can be found in the Old Testament principle that states, "The Lord your God led you all the way . . . in the wilderness, to humble you and to test you, to know what was in your heart" (Deut. 8:2). Christ was tempted in the wilderness, yet He knew the purpose of His needs. Jesus asked that question of Philip and that's why He left this story for all posterity—that we might be confronted with the question, too. What is the purpose of our needs?

Philip had a cash register for a mind. When Jesus asked him what they were going to do, Philip's first reply was that eight months' salary—more than 200 *denarii*—would not buy enough bread for everyone to have a little piece. His first thought was not the glory of God or the power of Jesus Christ. His first thought was, "How much is it going to cost?" He was not thinking of the miracles of God. Rather, he thought of the situation in earthly terms.

What was Jesus hoping he'd say? "Lord, I don't know, I don't know what we're going to do, but it's no problem for You. We've seen You turn water into wine; we know You can do anything when we factor You into the equation of life." Philip had been with Christ and seen the miracles He had performed. What was His purpose? Could it be that in the times of our greatest need, the Lord is saying to us, "Trust in Me. I will provide."

Finally, there was no sense of potential. Look at the boy for a moment: "There is a lad here who has five barley loaves and two fishes." That boy left home that morning with a little sack lunch of fish sandwiches. He left home that morning with the potential to feed thousands of people, and he didn't even know it. It's not the size of our lunch that matters, what really matters is who possesses it—whether Jesus has it or not—because little is much when God is in it.

THE GREAT PROVIDER

The above story demonstrates God's law of supply and demand. Without Christ, demand always exceeds supply, and the cry is, "Not enough!" All those people on the Galilean hillside who had not prepared created great demand; they needed something to eat. They were hungry, but there was not enough supply. So, what happened? Christ took the loaves and fishes and multiplied them. When we factor Jesus Christ into the equation of our lives, supply always exceeds demand. The cry changes from "Not enough!" to "More than enough!" Certainly that was true in this case. Christ fed the five thousand and twelve baskets full remained.

THE REAL BOTTOM LINE

What would we do if we ever found ourselves in a situation similar to Philip's? What if a young couple struggling to get out of school debts, and living off two incomes, suddenly discovers that the wife is pregnant? What if a natural disaster destroys your home, and it isn't covered by insurance? What if the company you work for suddenly lays you off? Most of us would find ourselves tabulating costs and estimating expenses. Yet in each of those situations, we might end up still not having our basic needs met.

During such stressful times, secrets faults can become agitated. Satan zeros in on us. The pressure to withstand sin increases dramatically. Satan tempts us with sinful ways to recoup our losses. We are tempted during a time of weakness, much like Christ in the desert, and our solution to this time of tempting is the same as Christ's in the wilderness—God's power.

Instead of giving into temptation, we must remember the incredible power of God. We should not be like the disciples, doubting the possibilities even after Christ clearly demonstrated His power before them. We must have faith in the promises of God to meet our needs and to do what is best for us. Paul tells us that since God's love did not even withhold His Son from us, He will not withhold anything else good from us, especially in our time of need. We must move closer to God, depending on Him more. Such faith and dedication will serve us regardless of our future, and we must realize the need to be prepared. We have responsibilities to God and our families which should prompt us to think about the future and not be left as startled as Philip.

We must be ready to answer questions similar to those asked of Philip. We need to ask ourselves about a plan, a purpose, and a potential for our own lives. Many times these essential questions are left unanswered, virtually ignored. We are so busy keeping up with all the other drivers on the highway, we don't realize we should be planning where we are going. Not just a specific plan for a specific event, like Philip needed, we need an overall plan, a vision. This vision is necessary for serving Christ through our ministry. We have a responsibility as good stewards of all that he has given us to give some thought to plans, purposes, and potentials as we serve the Lord with our lives.

However, as much as we may plan, at some point we must depend upon the power and the will of God. Just as there was a reason that Philip could not handle the situation he was in, we may find ourselves in a situation beyond our control. During such moments, God's ever-present power becomes explicitly known to us. Just as with the fish and the bread, no other resource but God using His power could produce the needed results.

We must remember that we are limited by our resources and corrupted by our sin nature, even if we are good stewards. God's infinite power is not limited by supply and demand. Although we must attend to our responsibilities, ultimately all rests in Him. We must place our hope and faith in His unrivaled power, mercy, and love.

When all seems hopeless, He is our hope. When there seems to be no way out, He is our way of escape. When we have little, He is our abundance. When we are devastated by a moral earthquake, He is our rescuer and restorer.

He is our All in All. That is not just good theology—it is also good economics.

Moral Soundings

- Are you a bottom-line person—to the point that you've worked God out of the equation?
- What does your checkbook reflect about what is important in your life?
- How much do you trust and seek the Lord to meet the needs in your life?
- Do you have a purpose or a plan about how to allocate your resources?
- What are your weak areas that Satan attacks during times of pressure?

Part Five:

THE GOD OF THE SECOND CHANCE: BEGINNING AGAIN

I am resolved no longer to linger,
Charmed by the world's delight;
Things that are higher,
things that are nobler,
These have allured my sight.
—Peter Hartsough

–17–

QUAKE PROOFING

Therefore everyone who hears these words of Mine,
and acts upon them, may be compared to a wise man,
who built his house upon the rock.
Matthew 7:24, NASB

಄

Early in 1995 an earthquake measuring 7.5 on the Richter scale struck the oil town of Neftegorsk on the island of Sakhalin, off the Pacific coast of Russia. Blocks of five-story apartment buildings collapsed, crushing hundreds of people. Of the three thousand people who lived in the town, about two thousand were killed.

Shoddy Soviet engineering contributed to the destruction. Although earthquakes are common in the region, the buildings in Neftegorsk were not built to withstand earthquakes. Because budget cuts had closed five of the island's six seismic stations, the city received no early warning. "We live from earthquake to earthquake," said Aleksei Nikolayev, director of the Center for Seismology and Engineering in Moscow. "Until something happens, no one does anything about it."

Today we can do a great deal to prepare for these geologic disruptions. We know how to build buildings that can withstand earthquakes. We have instruments that can detect signs of an approaching quake. But Neftegorsk did not use this knowledge. The city failed to prepare, and when the earthquake hit, the city was caught off guard.

In the same way that communities can prepare for the cataclysm of earthquakes, we can prepare for the catastrophe of moral earthquakes. We can build upon sturdy foundations—solid enough to withstand the worst disturbances imaginable. We can ensure the safety of those around us. We can quake-proof our lives simply by following the prescriptives of wise living outlined in the Scriptures.

X MARKS

The question is posed, "How can a young man keep his way pure?" (Psalm 119:9, NASB). At first blush, we might answer rather negatively. After all, we live in the midst of a culture that is literally wracked with seismic disturbances of monumental proportions.

More than one million teenagers will run away from home this year in America, many of them because of physical or sexual abuse in the home. This is America in the 1990s: one out of every ten teenage girls will get pregnant this year; half of all marriages will end in divorce, leaving hundreds of thousands of teenagers fearful of making commitments themselves later in life; and before the year is through half a million teenagers will attempt suicide.

The present generation faces an entirely different culture than the one in which their parents were raised. Our teenagers today are involved in a culture that is dragging them constantly down into a moral abyss. Young people beginning careers today are facing pressures they have never known before. It is a transition time for them. Others are leaving home for the first time, going off to college. They will be faced with increasing challenges: no one to check on them, living in coeducational dorms, no curfews, roommates—some with very different moral values—and all sorts of things taking place in the halls of their dormitories.

Other teenagers are entering high school or junior high for the first time. They will be faced with increasing pressures of wanting to be accepted, wanting to find their place, and trying to fit in with a world that has gone mad.

So the question the psalmist poses is as startlingly relevant today as when it was first penned, "How can we keep pure?" And the answer to that question is certainly no less urgent today than it was then.

NUTS AND BOLTS

The first word of the question *how* is typical of youth. It is a good question. How can I survive adolescence? How can I make it through these college years and stay pure in morals, pure in mind, and pure in my motives? How can I make it through this transitional change into this career while surrounded by temptations I never really knew existed? How can I make it through these teenage years when my body keeps changing, and I feel so dumb and insecure and hurt? How?

In the midst of all, God's Word speaks poignantly. The psalmist thus answers, "By taking heed according to your Word." He continues:

> *With my whole heart I have sought You;*
> *Oh, let me not wander from your commandments!*
> *Your word have I hidden in my heart,*
> *That I might not sin against You.*
> *Blessed are you, O LORD!*
> *Teach me Your statutes.*
> *With my lips I have declared*
> *All the judgments of Your mouth.*
> *I have rejoiced in the way of Your testimonies,*
> *As much as in all riches.*
> *I will meditate on Your precepts,*
> *And contemplate on Your ways.*
> *I will delight myself in Your statutes;*
> *I will not forget Your word. (Ps. 119:10–16)*

181

Young people and young adults are engaged in the most promiscuous culture known to the Western world, right here in America. Several factors come into play. The first is an element of intimidation. We have raised a generation in a public education system which has intimidated them intellectually into a belief in relativism—into accepting the absurd notion that everything is relative, that there are no moral absolutes. This intellectually indefensible position has given rise to all sorts of things, like coeducational dorms. For example, a preacher and his wife were sending their daughter to a school in the East. When they took her there to check into the dorm, they discovered it was coeducational. However, there was one floor that was reserved for only girls. Relieved, they were going to place her there until the dorm mother said, "Unless she's a lesbian, she doesn't want to be on this floor, because this floor is made up of lesbians." So she moved to a coeducational floor.

This is the way it is in many college campuses around America. There are few moral absolutes anymore. How can we keep pure in a culture that is telling our young people that no one can stay pure? It teaches them sex education from the time they are knee high, speaks very little—if any—about abstinence, and hands out condoms in secondary schools. How can we keep pure in a culture that keeps telling us we can't?

Well, it's not true. Young people can stay pure, and many do. The greatest gift young persons can give to their future husbands or wives is their own moral purity.

Isolation is another problem in today's culture. The urbanization of America, the move to the cities, has brought anonymity and loneliness. You'd think it would be just the opposite, but it is not. No one knows who you are, no one knows where you go, no one knows what you do, no one knows what you watch, and no one cares. You are away from those who care. Many children come home to houses that are empty after school. They sit in front of the television set and watch talk shows that are filled with degradation and blatant sexual talk.

Third, there exists an element of the counterfeit. It is all over this culture. There exists a lot of imitation role models, especially of families in our culture. They are called "families," but it is really a facade. One example is the "family" of a fourteen-year-old young man named Peter. His parents divorced when he was six years old. He lives with his mom, but spends weekends with his dad. He hates it because his dad's new girlfriend doesn't like him. Time with his mom is strained too. She remarried when he was nine; she had another little boy who is now four, then divorced again. Peter and his little half-brother get along well, but his half-brother is gone a lot visiting his dad. Peter's mom married a third time, and her new husband has two teenage kids who push Peter around and treat him badly. His mom and dad fight a lot on the phone—mostly over child support payments. His dad thinks they are too high; Peter says that makes him feel rotten and worthless. He notes that his daddy had money last year to buy a new sports car. He wonders if his dad really loves him, because he seems more interested in his new girlfriend. That's Peter's family. The name is the same—*family*—yet it is a hollow corrupted version of the word.

Fourth, there is the element of information—false information. The media has a negative influence on moral values. Recently, the front page of my hometown newspaper carried a big story on "a new kind of family," about two gay men and two lesbians who wanted to have children through artificial insemination, and they did. Then in the "Metro" section there was another big article on the gay lifestyle and the acceptability of it. Then, in the "Today" section of the same paper, another article advocated the acceptance of the gay lifestyle. It is overwhelming and morally wrong.

Lastly, there is the element of inculcation—impressing something upon the mind through repetitive, frequent repetition. Young people today are bombarded by advertising that tells them a hundred times a day that illicit sex is normal; that it ought to be the center of their lives. Consumerism teaches them to find satisfaction and hope in materialism and self-indulgence.

When many parents were teenagers, the moral climate was drastically different. They didn't have to deal with intimidation and relativism—the Ten Commandments were on the wall of public school classrooms. There were moral absolutes. They didn't have to deal with isolation. Everyone knew their neighbors. On my block we knew who lived next door to us. We knew almost everybody. In fact, if one kid did something wrong, the neighbors would take care of it, and dad would thank them for it later.

It is a challenging world out there. So the question is, "How can a young man keep his way pure?"

According to the psalmist, in the midst of all these cultural challenges, we have but one chance: to center our lives in the Word of God. He says, first of all, to keep the Word of God in your head. Know the Word. Second, he says to keep the Word of God in your heart. Stow the Word. Hide it there. Third, he says to keep the Word of God in your life. Show the Word by heeding the Word. Fourth, he says keep it on your lips, sow the Word with your mouth.

KNOW THE WORD

God's Word is a stable rock which we must use to support us. It is our foundation. We can keep ourselves pure. In your head, know the Word. "Blessed are You, O Lord! Teach me Your statutes" (Ps. 119:12). It is difficult for the Bible to impact your life if you know little about it. In school, you are taught information and then comes a test. If you don't know the material, you fail the test and eventually the course. The same is true of a football team. Each team member learns all the plays. If a player doesn't know the playbook, he won't know where he's supposed to go when the ball is snapped. He will be out of step, affect the whole team, and lose the game.

It is the same with the Word of God. The most important book in anyone's educational experience is the Bible, but it will do you little good if you don't study it. There are a lot of believers who say they love the Word but never study it, never learn it. How can you keep yourself pure? By saying, "Lord, teach me your statutes." In our head, we must know the Word. In the average church, if the preacher were to say, "Let's turn to Hezekiah," many people would start hunting, flipping through the pages. They wouldn't find it: it's not in there.

Every time we study the Bible we ought to pray with the psalmist, "Open my eyes, that I may see wondrous things from Your law" (Ps. 119:18). To fully understand God's Word, we need spiritual help. The Bible is a foreign language without the Holy Spirit's interpretation. We need to ask, "Lord, open my eyes this morning, that I will see wondrous things from your Word." Indeed, "Forever, O Lord, your Word is settled in heaven" (Ps. 119:89).

Some young people go to college where professors scoff at what the individual learned in church since nursery days. They are told, even in many so-called Christian colleges, that the first eleven chapters of Genesis are not historical. They are told that, at best, Jonah is an allegory. Yet long after those skeptics are gone, the Word of God will still stand true. As Isaiah proclaimed,

The grass withers, the flower fades,
But the word of our God stands forever. (Isa. 40:8).

There will be times when those going off to college may feel lonely, burdened, and rejected. During such times they may be tempted to go out with the wrong crowd and do things they shouldn't. Let those be times when, as the psalmist says, "When I was afflicted, it was good for me, for then I learned your statutes." Make up your mind that not a day is going to go by in your life that you don't expose your mind to the Word of God. How can a young person keep himself pure? In your head, know the Word of God.

BY HEART

Stow the Word of God in your heart. The psalmist said it well:

> *Your word I have hidden in my heart,*
> *That I might not sin against You. (Ps. 119:11)*

And again,

> *I will meditate on Your precepts,*
> *And contemplate Your ways. (Ps. 119:15)*

It's not enough to keep the Word in your head. You need to store it in your heart—memorize it, then meditate on it. Do you remember the instruction God gave Joshua? "This Book of the Law shall not depart from your mouth, but you shall meditate in it day and night, that you may observe to do all that is written in it. For then you will make your way prosperous, and then you will have good success" (Josh. 1:8).

Some of us are crossing over into a new land, like Joshua. And if that advice is good for those going into Canaan, it is certainly good for those going into college, those going into careers, and for all of us who wish to quake-proof our lives.

Meditate on the Word of God. Going over and over the Word deepens its impression. It is like a tune that we can't get out of our minds. Imagine what would happen if we couldn't get Scripture out of our heads. What would be the effect if we memorized Scripture daily? What would our witness be like if we always carried a Scripture memory card in our pocket?

Why not try this: for one month, stow the Word of God in your life. How? Take the Book of Proverbs and read through one chapter each morning. Thirty-one days in the month, thirty-one chapters in Proverbs. Whatever the day is you start reading, you start on that chapter. Keep it correlated with the day of the month, then you'll always know what chapter you're in. It will take five to ten minutes each morning. As you read that chapter, ask God to give you one verse to memorize. Write it down on a card and keep it in your pocket. Then when you're eating break-fast, take it out, read it, then put it back in your pocket. When you're at a stoplight, take it out, read it again, and put it in your pocket again. Do this as often as you can throughout the day. Meditate on it all day long. What will happen if you keep doing this all day with one verse? You will know it by heart. Then the next time temptation beckons, you will be prepared:

> *Your word I have hidden in my heart,*
> *That I might not sin against You. (Ps. 119:11)*

Why should we memorize Scripture?

> *You are my hiding place and my shield;*
> *I hope in Your word. (Ps. 119:114)*

When you memorize God's Word, it becomes a hiding place for you. And as we live each day in the fallen world, each one of us is going to need a hiding place in some way or another.

The psalmist says,

> *I have chosen the way of truth;*
> *Your judgments I have laid before me. (Ps. 119:30)*

We must make a choice to know God's Word. It doesn't come easy; it takes discipline. Yet if we want to keep ourselves pure: we must know the Word in our heads and stow the Word in our hearts.

Of course, there will be distractions, reasons why we should put off our Scripture reading. Plan for those times. Make an appointment with God each morning and don't break it—no matter what.

Remaining pure is a choice that we have to make. Daniel made that choice. It says that he purposed in his heart not to eat the king's meat. The psalmist made that choice:

> *With my whole heart I have sought you;*
> *Oh, let me not wander from your commandments. (Ps. 119:10)*

We must choose to build upon the solid rock of God's word. Noth-ing else is truly stable.

OUR SOLID FOUNDATION

If we base our lives on the ideas of our culture, we are like rock riddled with cracks, faults, and fractures. The rock crumbles under new pressures. It will not stand the test of time or the beating of the waves. The house built on that rock will fall, as if it were on sand. Yet if we build upon the Word of God, our house will stand forever. It rests on that solid faultless rock. Nothing the world has to offer measures up to this precious, infallible, and inerrant Word.

Moral Soundings

- How much time do you spend each day in the Word?
- Do you spend more time absorbing the ways of this world than in the Bible?
- Do you know the Word—do you aspire to thoroughly study it from cover to cover?
- Do you regularly memorize the Word?
- Are you building your house on the rock or on the shifting sand?

–18–

REACHING GENERATION X:
A NEW GENERATION FOR CHRIST

In Him we have redemption through His blood,
the forgiveness of sins, according to the riches of His grace.
Ephesians 1:7

৵

Throughout Christ's ministry we see Him continually offering the gospel, healing, and love to the sinners around Him. Even when the religious leaders of the day made remarks about this practice, He replied that only a sick man needs a doctor. Ironically, those religious leaders were some of the most notorious sinners around. Christ's delicate balance of love and boldness changed lives. His model of balance for ministry is an aspect desperately needed by many churches.

In our world today, beyond the walls of the church of Jesus Christ is an almost entire lost generation—lost to Christ and lost to His church. They have been raised in an unprecedented culture of moral ambiguity. They have been taught through their schools and in many of their homes that there are no ethical certainties, and, therefore, absolute truth doesn't exist. Yet we, the church of Jesus Christ, have a glorious commission from our Commander in Chief—a command from headquarters, a mandate from the Lord Jesus Himself. We are to reach out to that lost generation. Our commission is to go, make disciples, and teach them, baptizing them in the name of the Father and of the Son and of the Holy

Spirit. We have a heaven-sent commitment to reach the lost world.

Many churches are scrambling to do so. Yet some in their quest to make their message relevant, compromise the good news and sacrifice the message of the gospel. Pastors tell funny stories on Sunday mornings, yet their sermons remain little more than fluff because they never open the Word of God. The message they offer, devoid of any spiritual meat, lacks impact. These churches forget that Christ preached boldly before all, accepting the fact that not everyone would be happy and accept His message of godly truth. Christ realized that the sin nature in man would desire to reject and suppress that truth.

Others churches don't compromise, they condemn. So while an entire generation is lost outside the walls of the church, they sit inside, beat the Bibles, and scream in condemnation of the world. These churches are so indignant about the fact of unbelievers are sinning that love seems to evaporate in an isolationist us-against-them mentality. Like the Pharisees many seem to have a legalistic holier-than-thou attitude. These churches have forgotten that all have sinned and fallen short. Just because we're saved doesn't mean we're not sinners anymore.

Then there are the churches that neither compromise nor condemn. They condone. In their quest to reach a lost world, they simply condone immoral lifestyles. They refer to them as "alternative" lifestyles. These churches put a great deal of emphasis on the accepting love of Christ. They say He always loved, and never cared how a person acted. They preach a feel-good gospel: Jesus accepts you where you are, and we don't need to change you a bit—ever. These churches forget that once we come to Christ, we are to conform to Him, not make Him conform to us.

THE X GENERATION

We need to realize that this lost generation did not leave the church. In many ways the church left them. So we need to go back and get them. Our commission is to reach this unchurched generation. How do we do that? First we must know more about them. Studies and research name five common characteristics of this generation without Christ.

First: They are searching for meaningful relationships. Many in this lost generation have never really known a real relationship, and because of this, many of them are afraid of any kind of commitment.

Second: They don't want to wait for anything. They want it all now. They want immediate gratification.

Third: They want it for nothing. By and large, many of them haven't had to work for what they have, so they expect a free ride through the rest of life. The first thing that comes to many of their minds is this: *What's in it for me? Give it to me, but make sure you give it without cost and without condition.*

Fourth: They want guilt-free living. They've been raised with no moral absolutes. George Barna in his demographic studies says that 81 percent of them don't believe that there is absolute truth. If it feels good, they want to do it.

Fifth: They're searching for prosperity. They want it; they just don't have much hope of obtaining it. Most will not live in as nice a home throughout the rest of their lives as the home in which they were brought up. Their parents were brought up in the free love atmosphere of the sixties. They are brought up in a world full of AIDS. Their parents were brought up in an economic boom, so they are brought up in a world of downsizing and low-entry level jobs. They get their college degrees, then can't find any place to use them. They will have heartaches, struggles, and needs.

This lost generation struggles with problems most older adults know very little about. At a time when relativism is rampant in our country; at a time when churches are compromising, condemning, or condoning; at a time when social ills abound: What do we have to offer them? What do we have that they desire?

The answer is simple: We offer truth. We offer them the infallible and steadfast truth—the Word of God. They may believe that material gains are worth searching for; however, that is not the true focus of their search. Although they may not realize it, the focus of their search is an understanding of their own human hearts. This understanding can only be achieved in the true Word of God. It can only be achieved at the foot of the cross of Jesus Christ.

AT THE CROSS

What happened on the cross can only be understood in light of the Old Testament sacrificial system. All of the Old Testament sacrifices pointed toward the Lord Jesus Christ. He is pictured in the innocent little animal that was slain and whose skins were taken to cover the sins of the first man and woman. Adam and Eve watched that little animal breathe its last breath, shed its blood and die. They were the first to know the expensive toll that sin takes upon one's life. They knew that there is no remission except through the shedding of blood. When Abel brought his sacrifice, his offering of the first of his flocks—it was a picture of Jesus.

During the first Passover, every one of the Israelite homes was instructed to get a lamb, one that was pure and spotless. They were told to kill it. With a hyssop branch, they then spread the blood of the Passover lamb over the doorpost and lintel of their home, so that during night when the death angel visited Egypt, he would see the blood and pass over that house.

The blood of the Passover lamb meant deliverance from death and freedom from slavery. This was a picture of the blood of Jesus Christ. When Abraham was told to sacrifice on Mount Moriah, he offered his only son Isaac. Jesus was the substitutionary ram caught in the thicket to take Isaac's place.

The Bible says, "But now in Christ Jesus you who once were far off have been brought near by the blood of Christ" (Eph. 2:13). That is why Simon Peter said, "You were not redeemed with corruptible things, like silver or gold, from your aimless conduct received by tradition from our fathers, but with the precious blood of Christ, as of a lamb without blemish and without spot" (1 Pet. 1:18–19).

That is also why, when John the Baptist saw Him coming down to Jordan, he pointed his finger in our Lord's direction and said for all to hear, "Behold! The Lamb of God who takes away the sin of the world" (John 1:29). If there is one subject in the church that is ignored today, it is the blood of Jesus Christ. Many preachers speak platitudes and refer to the Sermon on the Mount, but few really preach about the sacrifice on the mount—the blood of Jesus Christ, God's Son, that cleanses us from all sin. Charles Spurgeon told the young preachers in his school that a true test of whether a man is preaching the gospel or not is the emphasis he makes on the blood of Jesus Christ.

What Christ has to offer us is freedom from guilt. "In Him we have redemption through His blood, the forgiveness of sins" (Eph. 1:7). That is what Christ has to offer us—the forgiveness of sins. Without that covering, sin will hound and haunt us. David said, "O, my sin is ever before me." When we come to Jesus Christ and let His blood cleanse us—Christ comes into our life and we receive the free gift of eternal life—written across our lives are the words of true liberty: "There is therefore now no condemnation to those who are in Christ Jesus" (Rom. 8:1).

What is guilt-free living? We live in a world ridden with guilt. Some of it is authentic. Some of it is artificial. Some of it is heaped on us by someone else. Yet at the same time, we have a society that is becoming desensitized. When there is no acknowledgment of God in a culture, in a school, or in a government, consequently there is no sense of sin.

That is why the anti-Christian forces want to remove the Ten Commandments everywhere. They don't want anybody praying at public events. Prayer in the schools is an acknowledgment of God. What happens when there is no acknowledgment of God? There is no sense of sin; and when there is no sense of sin, there is no need to be forgiven of anything, especially if there are no moral absolutes.

We need to remember that Christ offers us forgiveness. His forgiveness is not superficial. The word for forgiveness comes from a Greek word that literally means "to leave, to send away." A form of the same word is found in Matthew 4. It says that when the disciples saw Jesus, He called them to follow Him and they left their boats. They didn't look back. They never went back to their previous lives. They left. The same word is used in the Gospels in a story about a child with a fever. After Jesus' touch, the fever left—the same form of the word translated "forgiveness." Matthew 18 talks of a shepherd who left the ninety and nine? The word means "to send away or to leave." The word for sin is not the familiar word for sin which means missing the mark. It is a compound word in Greek from a preposition meaning "beside" and from a verb that means "to fall or to fall away from or to fall beside." Thus, for those of you who have stepped over the line, who have fallen down, who have fallen alongside, and fallen away, what does Jesus offer you? He offers to send away your sins.

The Old Testament sacrificial system speaks of a scapegoat. The priests would take the scapegoat out and send it away in the wilderness: "Send it away." That is what He wants to do with our sin. It is like a fever that goes away, or like men who leave their ship. He will send it away. That is what He offers—the forgiveness of sin.

We often have the wrong idea of forgiveness; but then, Jesus knew we would. That's why He gave us the story of the prodigal son. The wayward son went home in fear and trembling. He had prepared his speech to say, "I am no more worthy to be called your son." What was the father's response? "Bring a fatted calf!" The son received full reconciliation, as if it never happened. His sins were forgiven; his sins were forgotten.

Most people have a wrong concept of guilt. We often view it as our foe. Authentic guilt, if it is caused by something we have done, is not our foe. It is our friend. Guilt is sometimes God's way of saying, "You have sinned." Confession is our way of saying, "I agree." Those authentic guilt pangs—not the ones heaped on you by someone else, but those that come upon you by God's great providential power—are God's way of pricking your heart. In fact, the word *confession* used in this text, comes from a compound word that means "to say the same as God says." We like to pretend that we are not responsible. For example, when somebody sitting at a table knocks over a glass of ice tea, everybody jumps up and takes their napkins—except the guilty one.

So often that is the way we are with our sins. We cheat in business and God says, "What happened?" We say, "Oh, Lord, it was the pressure of the economy." We get in trouble on a Friday night, and God comes around and says, "What happened?" We say, "Oh, it was peer pressure. Everybody was doing it. " When someone runs off with somebody else and God says, "What happened?" They say, "Oh, it is just one of those things." It should not be this way. Confession takes responsibility. There is no forgiveness without confession. Confession says, "I agree with God." Guilt-free living comes only with confession.

What does Christ have to offer us? Christ offers us something purposeful, "In Him we have redemption through His blood, the forgiveness of sins, according to the riches of His grace" (Eph. 1:7). What Christ has to offer us is purpose. He is the only one who can fill the void of life. Some of us have been trying to fill the void with things or with money. All the money in the world can't fill that void. We try to fill it with cars or homes or people. All those things will never compare to the riches of His grace. What makes it all possible? The last word in the verse and the last word of the gospel: *grace*.

How can we know the riches of His grace? We discover the worth of something by knowing the price that we pay for it. When we buy a new car, the price we pay is what we think it is worth. Consider a painting? What about a house? We should never forget that the precious blood of the Lord Jesus Christ is the price of redemption. God did not send His own Son into the world because we kept pleading with Him to do so. Our redemption is entirely by His grace. "For by grace you have been saved through faith, and that not of yourselves; it is the gift of God, not of works, lest anyone should boast. For we are His workmanship, created in Christ Jesus for good works, which God prepared beforehand that we should walk in them" (Eph. 2:8–10). No wonder Paul, said, "For you know the grace of our Lord Jesus Christ, that though He was rich, yet for your sakes He became poor, that you through his poverty might become rich" (2 Cor. 8:9).

Moral earthquakes don't just happen! They are preceded by secret faults that run through one's life leaving cracks in character, which ultimately bring damaging and often devastating results. When left unchecked, these secret faults begin to converge and build pressure below the surface until they finally erupt into a moral collapse. But this need not be the result. God knows our weaknesses. He is rich in mercy; that is, we don't get what we do deserve. And He is full of grace; that is, we do get what we don't deserve. When given freedom in our lives to do so, He can make a way when there seems to be no way. Is *grace* the last word for you?

Moral Soundings

- New conditions may demand new methods, but not a new message. Do you believe that?
- The current generation is utterly lost. What will you do to reach it?
- At a time when moral earthquakes are rampant, will you hold out the great hope of Jesus?
- Do you see the connection between Old Testament sacrifices and Christ's ultimate fulfillment?
- Is *grace* the last word for you—on every subject?